Ben Trovato remains strictly anony
he is, we'd have to kill you. His first
Trovato Files, Will the Real Ben Trov
Ben Trovato, Stirred Not Shaken. He
the *Cape Times*.

Reviews of *Ben Trovato, Stirred Not Shaken*

"If you haven't yet encountered the Ben Trovato phenomenon, you have been missing out on some of the best social satire South Africa has to offer." – **Georgina Guedes,** ***Brainstorm***

"For those not familiar with, or converted to, the order of Trovato, the man fires off letters to those of power and influence. He asks provocative questions, makes odd requests and demands a response – sometimes including a R10 'incentive' to hurry things along, or put him at the top of the list (he records, of course, who pockets and who returns his R10) …

Stirred Not Shaken is a riot, and a fine addition to his previous two collections of letters." – **Janet Parker,** ***Business Day***

"Ben Trovato is a one-man Flying Circus and a master of the literary type." – **Murray Williams,** ***Cape Argus***

"Only a person with a sense of humour in permanent retirement would fail to appreciate Ben Trovato … there are no sacred cows." – **Samantha Bartlett,** ***Cape Times***

"Trovato has perfected the art of playing the fool."
– **Lucas Ledwaba,** ***ThisDay***

"[A] laugh a minute from cover to cover."

– Lauren Cohen, ***The Herald***

Reviews of *The Ben Trovato Files* and *Will the Real Ben Trovato Please Stand Up?*

"Trovato is completely cracked. Long may he last."

– Michele Magwood, ***Sunday Times***

"The literary equivalent of the Unabomber."

– Elliott Sylvester, ***Cape Argus***

"Trovato ... should be ashamed of treating pillars of our establishment as objects of ridicule." **– Jim Jones,** ***Business Day***

"A satirical masterpiece." ***– Elle***

"A delightful lesson in how to eloquently bamboozle anyone of your choosing." **– Ann Ussher,** ***Interval***

"Your irresponsibility in choosing to set this collected correspondence loose on an unsuspecting public cannot be overstated."

– Robynn Weldon, ***The Star***

"Does this man hold nothing sacred?"

– Gilbert Gonzo-Smythe, ***Argus***

"Highly entertaining ... will have you in fits of laughter."

– Trish Murphy, ***The Citizen***

Ben Trovato's Guide to EVERYTHING

ZEBRA

Published by Zebra Press
an imprint of Struik Publishers
(a division of New Holland Publishing (South Africa) (Pty) Ltd)
PO Box 1144, Cape Town, 8000
New Holland Publishing is a member of Johnnic Communications Ltd

www.zebrapress.co.za

First published 2004

1 3 5 7 9 10 8 6 4 2

PUBLISHING MANAGER: Marlene Fryer
MANAGING EDITOR: Robert Plummer
EDITOR: Ronel Richter-Herbert
TYPE DESIGNER: Natascha Adendorff
TYPESETTER: Monique van den Berg

Cover design by GroundCrew
10 Harries Street, Plumstead 7800, Cape Town
e-mail: Kinsman@icon.co.za

Set in 10.5 pt on 15 pt Meridien

Reproduction by Hirt & Carter (Cape) (Pty) Ltd
Printed and bound by Paarl Print, Oosterland Street, Paarl, South Africa

ISBN 1 86872 911 7

www.imagesofafrica.co.za
IMAGES OF AFRICA
PHOTO LIBRARY

Contents

introduction

Bastards.

The lot of you. How dare you? How dare you stand about with faces like rejected donor organs and expect me to come to your rescue? Well, this is the last time. The last time, I tell you.

Before embarking on this selfless endeavour, I spent some time alone with my literary agent in the splendid seclusion of a shady glen near my Sea Point home. Well, it is more of a copse than a glen. I think the locals call it that because there are always a couple of undercover officers from the drug squad hanging about at the strangest of hours. I suppose we all need a little enchantment in our lives from time to time.

My agent, who also doubles as my spiritual advisor, recommended that I write two separate books: one for men and another for women. That way, she said, everybody gets to benefit equally from my wisdom. I was sceptical and had my doubts. She saw me sitting there with a doubtful look on my sceptical face and, like the professional that she is, quickly pointed out that I would also make twice as much money from desperate losers of both sexes.

Things were going swimmingly until I broke for a light lunch. While munching on my hydroponically grown psilocybin and mung bean salad, I had a vision that bothered me tremendously. I packed my Arctic Trail tent and loaded up with tinned food and candles and incense and went up the mountain to think about things for a long, long time. I had been up there for almost a full hour before it hit me: *Men and women are from the same planet!* The realisation left me reeling. It is no exaggeration to say that I felt closer to that shiny eternal life force thingy than ever before. I quickly picked a fresh batch of liberty caps for dinner and headed for home shouting and laughing with joy. On my way down I passed Shady Glen being frisked by two narcotics agents, who told me to keep it down.

Back behind my shiny red Olivetti, I could see with great clarity (for the first time) that people who write self-help books are genuine altruists who care deeply about the human condition. I called up my spiritual advisor to expose her for the money-grubbing capitalist dog that she really is, but she quickly blamed her literary agent persona and went on in soothing tones to assure me that my reputation as a caring, sensitive man would not be harmed in the writing of this book. She said that authors of self-help books are not the pathological mountebanks that some people think they are. Oh, no. Instead, these public-spirited philanthropists choose to live modest lives, divvying up their royalties among the mental, physical and spiritual basket cases of this world.

So, the next time you pass a wine-soaked varmint slumped on the pavement, toss a few coins into his cup. It might just be John Gray working on his next book. Or me, for that matter. In which case I would prefer high denomination bank notes, if you don't mind. Coins generate such negative feng shui, even among the homeless.

How to make a woman fall in love with you

(without losing your self-respect, individuality and personal freedom)

Introduction

Unlike car keys, Love can never be lost forever. Like its duplicitous sister, Trust, it can only be misplaced. The only difference is that a late-night altercation with Trust can leave you with incisions that do not always heal in a straight line, while going ten rounds with Love can leave you with raw, jagged wounds that never heal at all.

I know people who would not think twice about choosing death over love. That's right. People who would rather die than fall in love again. One of my neighbour's cousin's best friends, Simon, first fell in love when he was fourteen. He is now forty-six with three ex-wives and a long line of girlfriends who would pay good money to see him chemically castrated on stage at the Bellville Velodrome. Three months ago, Simon left his 9-mm Parabellum in my neighbour's care, along with explicit instructions to shoot him down like a mad dog should he ever show signs of falling in love again. Neighbour Ted says because they are such good friends, he would feel compelled to carry out this mercy killing.

Anybody who has ever had to listen to a friend whose heart has been ripped out and stamped upon will know what I am talking about. Women perhaps more than men. There can be few things more depressing than waking up in the morning to find Lucy with her tear-stained face squashed up against the front window trying to see if you are inside so she can ruin your day by going on and on about that Craig bastard until you can take it no longer and excuse yourself so that you can take a shower just to wash the catharsis off.

Fronzi is an Italian half-caste friend of the family who has been in and out of love more times than I care to mention. He has an active social life, two semi-active cats and a loose circle of mostly inactive friends. His passion is getting women to fall in love with him. And he is very good at it, for the simple reason that he has learnt one important lesson: Be honest. Not to the women, of course. The ability to lie with integrity is an essential tool in the business of making a woman fall in love with you. Instead, he is honest with himself. Once he has got a woman to fall in love with him, he will confront himself and ask the question: "Do I love this woman?" The answer varies, but the course of action is always the same. But more on this later.

Gather round, boys and girls, because we are about to start the twelve-step programme on how to make a woman fall in love with you. Actually, girls, you might want to sit this one out.

Step 1 – Who are you?

I do not mean this literally. If you have ever had to refer to your driver's licence to verify your identification for your own peace of mind, this book is not for you. If you are searching for something to justify your life on any kind of existential plane whatsoever, then it is best that you take out a couple of magazine subscriptions. One to *Cosmopolitan* and another to *GQ* should do it. Perhaps throw in *Barely Legal* to ensure that you get all the answers you need. Good luck. I hope you find yourself.

What I mean is what *kind* of person are you? Love, like drugs and strong liquor, affects people in different ways. You have to be strong to cope with love. I do not want to be held responsible for any emotional drownings. I have enough trouble on my hands as it is. Like Africa, love is not for pussies. Do not come to me later with your thin-lipped lawyer whining about damages. I will destroy you. Now, back to love.

More than ever before, men want to know how to make a woman fall in love with them. The reasons for this are complex and often very disturbing. The truth is that men have grown increasingly insecure in the face of the total female onslaught. Everywhere around them, they see women no longer bothering to suppress their superiority. The archetypal helpless female is not only showing that she can change a fan belt, but she has had it studded with pop rivets and is now wearing it as a choker. She changes tyres as smoothly as she changes men. She snarls when doors are opened for her and smiles when she is dumped. And, in the face of this unprecedented reversal of fortunes, men have no choice but to turn to the very source of their pain and confusion for solace. Well, they do have a choice, but it is too horrible to consider. None of it makes any sense. And yet it all makes perfect sense.

But back to determining who you are, a crucial first step in finding true love. Right from the outset it is important to ascertain one thing: Are you gay? If so, you may find this section to be less than helpful. Unless you are a lesbian, of course, in which case everything still applies. Simply switch all the boy names for girl names. And everyone thinks same-sex relationships have to be complicated.

If you are not sure of your sexuality, I suggest you follow the aforementioned Magazine Method to determine who and why you are. Subscribe to *Playboy* and *Playgirl*. All will become clear the moment you find yourself reaching for one more frequently than the other. It really is that simple, and a whole lot cheaper than all those electro-convulsive treatments that you have been having.

Next, are you absolutely certain that this is what you want? Having a woman fall in love with you is not a matter to be trifled with. It is damn serious for all concerned. If you are unsure it is love you are feeling, go somewhere quiet where you can be alone with your thoughts. A deserted beach is fine. Once you have made sure there are no muggers around, close your eyes and think about the object of your desire. If you find yourself reaching into your trousers before you have even got the colour of her eyes pinned down, then it is most probably lust. But do not worry. Lust is good. Lust is as essential to love as the black ball is to a game of pool.

However, if you find yourself thinking about the way her hair blows in the wind or the way her eyes sparkle when she laughs or anything else that makes you want to write bad poetry, then it may very well be love. Unless, of course, you have just ingested a gram of methylenedioxymethamphetamine and are suffused with an overpowering empathy for animals, cars, rocks, trees, the universe and so on. In which case, straighten out and try again later.

We might be jumping the gun a bit here. First, you have to physically identify the woman you wish to fall in love with you. It is important that you select a real woman. Altogether too many men these days fall in love with unattainable women like Lara Croft and her digitally enhanced counterpart, Angelina Jolie.

The problem here is obvious. The object of your desire has never set eyes on you. You saw her for the first time in a nightclub or in the second-hand bookshop. In the 7-Eleven or the doctor's waiting room. You caught a glimpse of her in the back window of a passing taxi. Tanning topless at Llandudno. In the Autobank queue. Waiting for the elevator. Buying the *Cape Times* on a street corner in the teeth of a south-easterly gale. You looked up, and there she was. Then she wasn't. But in that instant, you fell in love. And this is where we start.

Step 2 – The first move

The first move is where it all begins. This is the genesis of love. The embryo of ecstasy. The nucleus of naughtiness.

The fountainhead of fun. The first move is what it all boils down to. Without the first move, you are doomed to spending the rest of your life in the company of the joyless Mrs Palmer and her five sullen daughters.

Men share many common experiences while growing up. One of them is projectile vomiting out of a car window at 120 km/h. Another is encountering a woman who makes the blood drain from your face. The problem is that all this blood has to go somewhere, so when your paths cross and you find yourself standing there with what is known as a *wistful* look upon your pale face, you have to move fast.

When you see a woman who makes your pupils dilate and you do nothing more than sigh *wistfully*, a terrible thing has happened. You have allowed something called *yearning* to enter your heart. Yearning is not good. It is the enemy of Love. It is a member of the Hate family, albeit a distant cousin.

There is only one thing worse than yearning, and that is melancholy. I don't even know what comes after melancholy. Probably a hosepipe through the back window of your rusting Hyundai. The fact that you are reading this suggests that you have not yet gone beyond melancholy. And this is encouraging. It means you still have hope. All you lack is courage. And maybe one or two social skills.

For shy men, the first move is a terrible thing. I know this because I was a shy man once and it got me nowhere at all. Shyness is an unbearable burden to bear. It simply doesn't work on any level whatsoever. If the meek have not inherited the earth by now, I find it highly unlikely that they ever will.

For a shy man, the ability to hold your alcohol is vital to a successful first move. It used to be plain old courage, but global warming and feminism have left men with dangerously thin skins. Men can no longer tolerate the same levels of rejection that they could ten years ago, so they have had to learn how to tolerate large amounts of alcohol instead. Across the world, rivers of vodka, brandy and cheap red wine are greasing the wheels of social intercourse. There are more shy alcoholics today than ever before, and there is a school of thought that says women are to blame for this.

The first move has the capacity to turn strangers into lovers. It is also capable of turning incredibly ugly, very quickly. To avoid public violence, there are certain basic rules to follow. Once you have spotted the woman without whom you shall surely die, make sure that she is alone. Many boyfriends, and even some husbands, have a problem with a stranger walking up to their woman and asking for a dance or her phone number or unprotected sex in the toilets.

Once you are certain she is alone, you can begin showing obvious interest on a visual level. In other words, make sure she notices you looking at her. At this point, it is important to ensure that your mouth is shut. It does not matter how beautiful she may be, do not sit there slack-jawed and drooling into the peanuts. This is not attractive. Be cool. Furrow your brow quizzically. If you are fool enough to have had a botox injection, find something else to furrow. Women like to feel mysterious. Actually, if they ever find out what a mystery most men find them, they might think of easing up a little in that department.

Keep your eyes on her. If you have good eye–hand coordination, raise a solitary eyebrow and at the same time take a slow hit of whatever it is that you are drinking. It is also important to be drinking something that the object of your desire will not find disturbing. A giant turquoise cocktail with a tropical nativity scene nestling on top will distract her. It will also get her thinking. So when she does smile at you, it will be because you have made her think of Sheldon, her best gay buddy in the whole wide world. You may as well leave immediately.

You can't really go wrong with a glass of beer – unless you happen to be an enormous bloated pig of a man, of course. Beer suggests that you are a man of the people. A tough, straight-talking, blueish-collar kinda guy. It is important not to rush your beer. Take it slowly. Savour it. Avoid gulping. Gulping can be very unattractive in certain environments. Try not to do it anywhere outside Munich in October. A gulper is a man who likes to finish things quickly. Any women seeing this will automatically draw one parallel, subconsciously or otherwise, and she will not want to go to all the trouble of taking her clothes off only to be putting them back on thirty seconds later.

Tequila will attract a certain breed of woman. Mexican, mainly. But if you happen to live north of the border, you will find that walking up to the bar and saying: "Got any gold?" will attract a certain amount of attention. If you live on the Reef, you run the risk of alerting the narc wearing his favourite false moustache and Gold & Diamond Unit shoes at the far end of the bar. But anywhere else, the request is likely to get you noticed by a woman who runs with the wolves. If wild is what you are looking for, keep drinking tequila. Not for the entire evening, of course. If she hasn't approached you by the time you feel your brain starting to melt, then switch to something else. Whisky is good. Women hate the smell of it, but if you are ordering Johnny Walker Blue at R100 a shot, most of them will be prepared to overlook the high-octane stench pouring from your mouth.

Another way of getting her attention is to ignore her completely. Women hate being ignored almost as much as they hate being hit on. As the Americans say, go figure. Again, cool is everything. Look into the middle distance as much as possible. The middle distance does not include faces, breasts or groins. It can be the ceiling. But too much of that can create the impression that the drugs have just started kicking in. Actually, avoid the ceiling. Studying parts of your own body is acceptable. It gives the impression that you are introspective. Again, avoid studying anything that might disturb the other patrons.

Gently moulding the top of a lighted candle can be very alluring. It suggests that you have depth. Try not to scream when molten wax erupts down your forearm. Nobody likes a wuss. If the venue does not have candles, bring your own.

Try to avoid ignoring her so effectively that three hours pass before you even notice that she has left.

If two unattended girls walk up to the bar, listen in on their conversation. Not only does this provide you with a valuable inside edge, but it also spares you the embarrassment of trying to explain in sign language that you don't understand Swedish. You might need to get in quite close, because there are still a handful of women out there who use normal sound levels to communicate with one another. If the music is very loud, do not attempt to lip-read. Men who watch women's lips while they are talking are thinking about one thing only, and there is a very good chance that women are aware of this. Your cue to jump into the conversation is when you hear key words like "rugby", "divorce" and "vulnerable". If your key words have not come up in the first hour, start looking out for words like "and", "but" and "if".

Assuming all goes according to plan, you have now caught the attention of the most desirable woman you have ever set eyes upon. Now what? This is the difficult part. If she is waiting for you to make the first move, no amount of fiddling with candles is going to help.

What you decide to do next could change the course of your life. Making the first move will get you out of the garage, into first gear and on the road to making her fall in love with you. Of course, it can also get you into the biggest bunch of trouble you could ever imagine. But never mind that right now.

Step 3 – The first words

Some books suggest that it is not important what you say. That the key is to say something. Anything. That the point is to simply make that initial contact. This is a lie. Those first words are critical. They will mark you forever.

A woman can remember what shoes you were wearing when she first met you. She can remember how many beers you had on your first date and she can remember what was playing on the radio when you dropped her off at her place afterwards. She can remember what the weather was like the night you made love for the first time. So you can be pretty damn sure that she is going to remember your first words to her. If women had memories like men, it would be less important for you to choose your words that carefully.

Throughout the evolution of modern man (1975–2004), there have been women standing with one eyebrow raised and a hand on the hip: "Are you telling me that you don't remember?" Cornered, we turn sullen. We become skulking dogs, sick at the thought of having nowhere to run. It is futile to try to busk your way through, because any attempt at feigning a sudden recollection is swiftly followed by a string of questions designed to break you down and force you to admit that: "Okay! I don't remember! Okay? Jesus. It's not the end of the world!" By now you are so traumatised that you can barely remember your way to the bedroom. That's the end of the conversation and you slink off, painfully aware that for the next few weeks all you will be licking are your wounds.

While it is vitally important to choose your first words and remember them and remember her reply and what she was drinking and what skirt she was wearing and whether or not a soft rain was falling, it is equally important to remember her name when you first meet her. There are only a certain number of times that a woman is going to respond politely to the question: "Sorry, you are ...?" Especially if she claims to have told you her name three times already. You could try blaming the tequila. But if she is not a wolf, it's not going to wash. Actually, if she is a wolf she is not going to care too much what you call her. As long as it's not Jane.

Repeatedly forgetting her name will eventually make her forget your name. She will start calling you Drunk. Do not argue. Accept the name and push on. Or push off, depending on the look on her face.

The first words used in the first move should be dictated by what the woman is doing with her face. Watch her closely as she interacts with her friends. That's assuming she is with friends. If she is alone, she could be with the police. Or she might be a hooker. Either way, you are going to end up paying dearly should you decide to make the first move.

But assuming she is what you think she is, keep your eyes on her for a few minutes. If she is the bubbly one in the group, the one who regularly shrieks with laughter and flicks her tresses hither and yon, then it is best not to approach her with lines like: "Do you believe that when someone says 'I breathe, therefore I am' and purports to demonstrate his existence from the fact that breathing could not exist without it, he demonstrates nothing at all, for he would first have had to prove that it is true that he breathes, and this is impossible without also having proved that he exists?"

It's a long shot, but she may well respond with: "What do I think? I think you're putting Descartes before Des Horse." If she does, then you've met your soulmate. Congratulations. However, it is far more likely that she will tell you to fuck off.

Once you are sufficiently intoxicated to make the first move, it is important to make sure that she doesn't see you coming. Blindside her if you can. You do not want a situation where she notices you the moment you stand up on the other side of the room and begin walking purposefully towards her. She is not going to smile encouragingly and wave you over. Her eyes are going to widen in what you correctly assume to be horror. Then she will lower her head and turn slowly to her friends. They will all swivel in their chairs to look at you. Against all the laws of physics, you will find yourself walking in slow motion. Everyone, apart from the goddess, is staring at you. Then all of her friends will collapse in hysterics, as if somebody at the table has just said something incredibly funny. At this point you have two choices: Allow nothing to deviate you from your mission, knowing that by losing the element of surprise you run the risk of being crushed beneath an avalanche of biting put-downs when you reach her table. If you are feeling confident and on top of your game (the Nigerian never ripped you off, for once) and you are convinced that you will have a witty comeback for anything they might throw at you, then go right in. The regret will be almost instantaneous. Your second choice is to change direction. This is a problem if her table is in the corner and you are quite clearly headed for nowhere else but the corner. All you can do then is stop, narrow your eyes and look down. Give yourself a sharp slap on the forehead, turn and walk quickly away. Make for the exit. This creates the impression that you have just remembered you have a patient lying in theatre waiting for open-heart surgery. It could also create the impression that there is something seriously wrong with you. But since you can never again return to this place, what do you care?

Given the hazards of forewarning, it is far wiser to approach by stealth. This catches her off-guard and significantly increases your chances of getting her to fall in love with you. There is a reason why lions stalk their prey instead of hanging around on the fringes of the herd flexing their haunch muscles and tossing their manes in the hope that a gullible young springbok will come on over for a closer look.

The direct approach has its drawbacks. On many occasions throughout history, a man's opening gambit has led to bloodshed. Bars have erupted in violence through a misplaced word. Every hospital in the world has a small quota of male patients lying in traction, wondering what it was that they said.

But despite the inherent dangers, the direct approach has an impressive success rate. Depending on where you are, of course. You may not want to try it in a local taverna in a small fishing village on a remote part of Crete. Especially not if the seventeen glasses of retsina you drank for courage are making you speak in a thick, guttural slur that could easily be mistaken for German. But it might well work in an all-night subterranean absinthe bar in Pamplona's *barrio gottica* at the frenzied height of the San Fermin festival.

There are many, many words to choose from when deciding on your opening line. Dictionaries are full of them. But the secret lies in choosing the right ones and then stringing them together in a sequence that makes sense. All too often, men forget these basic guidelines and go in with a mish-mash of mixed metaphors and crippled syntax. Nothing turns a woman off faster than a man who dangles his participles in public. You don't have to be Shakespeare. (Actually, that's a bad example. Nobody I know has the foggiest idea of what he was on about.) But you don't have to be Mike Tyson, either. I have overheard men approach women with lines like: "Hey, babe, you're like a … you got … psshhhh, you … I just want to … ay … know what I mean?"

There has to be an element of persuasiveness in every

opening gambit. Women no longer trust men, so they have to be persuaded to do pretty much everything from making the bed to making love. And this takes eloquence and a nimble mind.

At the best of times, men are hopeless when it comes to explaining themselves. Even when they have done nothing wrong. This is why women have evolved into such good listeners. They know that they have one shot at catching it. If they miss it the first time round, they run the risk of getting a completely different version because now the man has had time to revise his original statement. Then the woman is beholden to say: "That's not what you said …" and you have to respond with: "I thought you never heard me …" and this kind of exchange should happen after ten years of marriage, not ten minutes of conversation.

It is vital that you tailor your words to fit not only the woman, but the circumstances too. Recounting your first experience with anal sex inside a disused abattoir just as she sinks her teeth into her cheeseburger is not going to be appreciated. Be sensitive. Remember, you are not simply giving her a line so that you can score a quick shag. As I have pointed out, this is not that kind of book. You want her to fall in love with you. You want to be with this woman for the rest of your life. You wish you had ovaries so that you could have her babies. Never tell her this, of course. Ovary envy is just too weird for most women to handle.

To know which words to use, you have to know the different categories into which women fall. Only then can you accurately match the words to the women. Mismatching can be disastrous. It often leads to marriage and then later, when she realises that she completely misunderstood what you said when you first met, homicide or divorce. This is something you want to avoid.

Some typical genres of modern women

THE BITCH

Recent supervised studies undertaken in Switzerland have shown that bitchiness is a genetic trait in all women. Apparently it clings to oestrogen like a sucker fish to a shark as it courses through the body.

Bitches have to be watched like hawks. Turn your back on them for a moment and they have not only destroyed your self-confidence, but they have destroyed your chances with every other single girl within a 500-kilometre radius. As a man, your reputation and your erection are all that you really have going for you. The Bitch will not hesitate to destroy either, and all she needs to do it is her mouth.

I am not saying that you should avoid a woman simply because you detect a little Bitch in her. If that were the case, you may as well slip into a pair of silver spandex lederhosen and wander the slopes of Table Mountain yodelling in the hope that your soulmate will find you.

If you come across a Bitch who you think needs to fall in love with you, then you should be armed with more than a quick wit and a crumpled Rough Rider in your back pocket. Any woman with too much Bitch riding in her oestrogen has invariably had a recent encounter with a Bastard. Bastard is a genetic trait found in all men, but more on that later. This does not mean that the Bitch hates men. Far from it. All it means is that she is provoking you into some sort of reaction so that she may more fully get the measure of you as a man. This is interesting territory, and I would urge any man who finds himself in this situation to press on and not give up and walk away mumbling "bitch" under his breath, however tempting it may be. She will brand you a chickenshit mollusc and word will spread quickly. It is far better to take her on. Some adults say mind games are childish and that they have no time for them. However, they only say this because they do not know how to play. Mind games, like all the best games, have no rules. Small wonder, then, that the anally retentive among us scorn what they regard as a trivial pursuit. Mind games test your wits and, if played properly, make your partner question her sanity. This is good for any relationship, and let nobody tell you otherwise.

Since the Bitch will be analysing and appraising you according to the way you respond to her disagreeable manner, it is vital that you take a tack diametrically opposite to the one that you would normally take. Once she thinks she has you sewn up, you can begin letting bits of the real you leak out. Keep a serviette handy.

Bitches are easily confused because their mean-spiritedness

is often no more than a cheap glossy varnish on vulnerable bits that have grown tender and sore after too much exposure to, well, to men like you, I suppose.

THE BIMBO

The Bimbo is a woman who has successfully managed to mutate her Bitch gene into something more useful. Not many people know this, but the word originates from the ancient Uzbek phrase "bim", meaning "stupid", and "bo", meaning "goddess". The inherent contradiction goes a long way towards explaining why this former Soviet republic is in the state that it is today.

To be honest, few Bimbos will be found signing up for classes at the Massachusetts Institute of Technology. But they can certainly be found playing pool in some of the best pubs around Harvard Square. I have seen them with my own eyes. In fact, I spoke to a couple of them while I was in Cambridge wrapping up some unfinished business, and I can tell you that while they are not stupid, they certainly haven't done much reading. But this is no reason to condemn them. Three-quarters of the population of Africa has not read a book, and does the rest of the world shun and ignore them? Okay, bad example.

Bimbos exist for several reasons, one of which is to offset the number of ugly people in the world. Even amateur metaphysicists know that every action has a reaction, and there is no reason why this should be any different. It is all about balance. How sad it would be if all we ever saw were ugly women. The world is already full of poor people and they make a depressing enough sight for those of us with money. Bimbos are like songbirds on a cloudy day. They are sunspots on a stormy sea. They are pools of warm honey for the badgers of this world. But more about badgers later.

THE HIPPY

If you have your heart set on a Hippy, it is important to ascertain that she is genuine. There are many women out there who dress and act like Hippies, but they are not real Hippies. They do this for several reasons, one of which is to attract men who are attracted to Hippies. These kinds of men are generally well read and sensitive and know how to tell their oyster mushrooms from their liberty caps. They are in touch with the planet and they can access their inner child on demand. They can raise kids, corn and kundalini with equal measure. But only if they are genuine. And this is where things often fall apart.

There are plenty of non-Hippy men out there pretending to be Hippies so that they can snare themselves a Hippy woman. This is because Hippy women (if they are genuine) are into unfertilised eggs, unpretentious clothing and unprotected sex. In a world full of Bimbos and Bitches, this is frequently seen as a refreshing alternative. However, what sometimes happens is that a pseudo-Hippy man will charm the Indian skirt right off a fake Hippy woman, and it takes years before they realise that neither of them have been inhaling and that both of them prefer actuarial science to organic vegetables. They are harmless, but you don't really want them as your friends.

If you want to find out if your Hippy is real or not, the acid test (well, that too) is to ask her if she voted in the last election. Real Hippies reject all political systems because they are based on authority and control, anathema to the true flower child. Of course, there is always the danger that your Hippy turns out to be a bomb-happy anarchist who would be caught dead in a polling booth. Ah, what the hell. If she smells good in patchouli oil, go for it.

THE BOSS

If you are in a bar, she will be the one ordering the drinks, harassing the waiter for being too slow, and deciding who drinks what. She will also be the one making a very deliberate point of ignoring you.

Bosses have a tendency to come across as extremely asexual, much like garden snails. What a pity, then, that they don't shrivel up and foam at the mouth when their lips touch the salted rim of their pretentious margarita glasses.

If it is a Boss you are looking for, then the odds are that you are suffering from some sort of hormonal or mineral deficiency. Controlled studies have shown that, like the Bitch, all women have varying degrees of the Boss in them. It is contained in that spare X chromosome that makes them women. Most have been trained to suppress this gene, but the training is wearing thin with every new generation.

We have all heard the expression: "She Who Must Be Obeyed". But what started off as a B-grade movie joke has turned into an A-grade nightmare for every red-blooded male who grew up under the impression that he was in charge. Some self-help books say that apportioning blame does not help. I have never heard such rubbish in my entire life. If we all went around not blaming each other for the terrible things that happen, what kind of world would that be? I will tell you. It would be a world where nobody takes responsibility for their actions. Hang on. That's exactly the kind of world I want to live in. I will have to rethink this bit.

Domination is not necessarily a bad a thing, but it has its place. Its place is not in the kitchen making sure that the dishes are cleaned properly, nor is its place outside on the stoep nagging for the lawn to be mown. Its place is not following you around the house shouting at you for having come home drunk at three in the morning. I think it is a crying shame that these domestic dominatrixes can be found everywhere except in the bedroom.

If you really want a Boss, in addition to the penishead who controls you at work, then at least make sure you get one who will allow you to order the wine at dinner. Even if you can't tell an unwooded Chardonnay from an Augusto Pinochet, insist on ordering the wine. Be brave. If necessary, use your steak knife to fight her for the wine list. Remember that the Napoleonic wars could not have been fought and won without the first ship casting off.

THE PUSHOVER

She looks like a real-life animation from a warm, fuzzy Disney film. She is soft at the edges and has big eyes that stare in wonderment at everything that happens around her. When getting to know her, it is important to make sure that she is not afflicted with that disease that makes one's eyes big and staring.

The Pushover is often quite small and pretty in the face area. While the rest of the table hurls abuse at the blind rose seller, she rather sheepishly buys a flower. She has the look of a peasant girl who is about to fall in love in a Merchant-Ivory movie. There is a dreamy quality about her. She has never been hurt by a man. The Pushover is often a virgin once removed. Actually, often removed quite inadvertently by riding her favourite horse a little too hard. She might even have slept with one or two men, and has known nothing but amicable endings. Put on the kid gloves, the gentle smile and make your approach. No, that would be predatory. It would be like canned hunting and we all know there is very little sport in that.

Come to think of it, I have no advice for anyone wanting a Pushover to fall in love with them. I think you simply want to push her over and fall on top of her. And this is not that kind of book. Go and find another one, you sick puppy. Try the Religion section. At least you might find redemption.

THE DESPERADO

The Desperado will be making eye contact with every remotely eligible man in the place. It is likely that she has recently been dumped and is on the rebound. You have the advantage because she is vulnerable. Make use of it before someone else does. Her self-esteem has taken a beating, and you are just the person to give it back to her.

Desperados make good lovers because they try that much harder to please. No matter how tempted you may be, never abuse their generosity. Remember that deep down, they still harbour unresolved feelings of resentment towards men. When it comes time to deal with that, it is best to agree with everything she says. All men are bastards. That includes you. Swallow your pride and go with it. Hang your head in shame. Pay for the sins of men. Try to avoid developing a Messiah complex. You will have to convince her that you are not like the rest of them, and certainly nothing like that swine who stole her heart, used her body and disappeared with all the negatives. It won't be easy. There may even be times when you think that she is showing an altogether unnatural interest in your sister. Be strong. Unless you actually catch them in bed together, you are still in with a fine chance of landing the Desperado of your dreams.

THE JOCKETTE

Some men find gym bunnies terribly cute. Personally, I find them disturbing aberrations of nature. Men need to be physically strong to be able to run the world and remove beer bottle tops with their teeth. Women do not need muscles. Besides, the female metabolism is designed to work at a different rate to that of the male. Women can get all the exercise their bodies need through sex and housework. It's how much effort they put into it that counts. Some men cover their bedroom walls with mirrors to convince their wives that even if they are not having much fun they are still getting a good workout, so the hour is not completely wasted.

The gym is a relatively modern invention (*circa* Richard Branson). In the old days, women were built to chop wood and carry two children on each hip. They were big, no doubt about it, and men expected nothing less. Skinny women were avoided because there was a very good chance that they had the Black Plague. Or, worse, they did not know how to cook.

At some point, women began watching what they ate and started exercising. The catalyst for this behavioural change remains shrouded in mystery, although neighbour Ted believes that women began losing weight and working out around the time that beer was discovered. His reasoning is that the male hunter, a lean, well-built specimen, would return from a day of slaying wild beasts and fall upon the generous folds of his fleshy woman. Then one day his woman whipped up a whole new batch of soup made from malt, sugar, hops and water. The next day he had his mates round, and it wasn't long before all the women in the tribe were making soup around the clock. Soon enough, the wild beasts began openly sniggering at the sight of the hunter dragging his enormous belly around the bush. Returning home once again empty-handed, he tried to fall upon his corpulent woman and bounced right off. They were both so fat that even when they had their bodies pressed together, their rude bits were still a good half-metre apart. The man flatly refused to give up his soup, so it was left to the woman to shed her load. She trimmed right down, took a young lover and went on to become the editor of the first primitive women's magazine. The rest is history.

THE LESBIAN

Only a very small fraction of women are Lesbians as a result of eating genetically modified foods. Most are Lesbians either because it is trendy, or because they cannot bear the thought of facing another naked man. But, if you have the misfortune to pick on a mutant, there is not much advice I can give you. Keep your guard up and protect your groin. Don't try to run. Back away slowly.

If, however, it is the more common Type B Lesbian that has caught your attention, then you are in with a splendid chance of getting her to fall in love with you. The real challenge in trying to get her to go home with you lies in your approach. For a start, you are going to have to be very, very sensitive. Rodney, an ex-guitarist with a band that only ever played one gig in public, told someone who told me that he had a friend whose cousin told him that he was sensitive to a woman once and that it almost got him killed. There was probably more to the story, but I can't remember what it was. Anyway, that's not the point. The point is that to snag the Type B Lesbian, you are going to have to dig down deep and unleash your inner woman. A word of warning: Do not try to fake it.

Type B Lesbians are masters when it comes to superficiality, and they will not hesitate to crush your kneecaps and stomp on your crumpled body should they realise that you are working a con. You have to suppress every vestige of your masculinity and relate to them on an entirely different level. Only then will they open up enough to allow you to take them home and play gentle music to them and whisper soft words and massage their feet until their defences are sufficiently lowered for you to move slowly southward. Essentially, you have to pretend to be a woman trapped in a man's body. This is the only way you are going to win their trust. It is not as difficult as it sounds. Any moron can memorise a few lines of Dorothy Parker's poetry or learn how to write a haiku while taking a pee at the same time. It's only three lines, for God's sake. How hard can it be? You also have to make your hands and lips very soft. Aloe juice works for some. I was in this position once but there was no aloe juice around, so I used the juice of the Agave cactus instead. A word of warning: Even though tequila is a close relative of the aloe family, it will not do much for your lips. It will, however, make other parts of your body soft.

Gregoire, a French expatriate friend of somebody I met purely by chance in a Sea Point supermarket just as it was closing, said he had once met a Type B Lesbian in a nightclub, and was completely blown out of his culottes by the way she danced. Being French, he had no trouble getting in touch with his feminine side, and within seven hours he was licking the last of her lower back and offering to make fluffy omelettes for the two of them. Then, when it came time to get dressed and go home, he couldn't face putting on his coarse Levi jeans and instead began rifling through her skirts.

Look, I am not homophobic. Some of my best friends are as bent as paperclips. All I am saying is, be careful out there. If you are going to get in touch with your feminine side, make sure you know the way back home.

THE BASKET CASE

She is the one constantly checking her watch for the time and her cellphone for messages. Her eyes dart nervously around the room. She laughs a lot. Mostly at the wrong times. If you watch really closely, you will see her sneak a quick gnaw on her nails. She seems to be neurotic, but you can never be sure about these things. She could just as well be on the finest amphetamine sulphate this side of Silicone Valley. But despite the twitches and tics, she is quite the most exquisite creature you have ever set eyes upon. A friend will lean over and whisper something in her ear. She will collapse with laughter. Her whole body is convulsed with laughter. After a while it looks like she might actually be sobbing. But despite the warning signs, you can't help yourself. You bolt your drink and go over to talk to her.

She comes across like a highly strung racehorse that can't bear the feeling of a jockey on its back, and yet can't live without it. Proceed with caution. Try to find out why she is so jittery. Nine times out of ten, she is bordering on hysteria after staying awake for three straight nights because Roger dumped her for no reason at all and now he won't return her calls. Either that, or she is out of lithium.

If she tries to explain her behaviour on the grounds that she is menstruating, excuse yourself and pretend to go and buy a drink. When you reach the door, run like hell. There is no proven physical cause for any psychiatric disorder, and anyone who says otherwise is lying through their teeth and cannot be trusted with your heart.

THE VIRGIN

Can be difficult to identify, unless you are accompanied by one of those Zulu matriarchs whose job it is to check that teenage girls are intact before allowing them to participate in the rain-making ceremony. Even then, it is unlikely that she will agree to cooperate. Especially if the bar is crowded.

The best thing about Virgins is that they do not know the difference between good sex and bad sex. So, if you do manage to snare one, make sure that she never has an affair. The only way to do this is to lock her up in a tower and make sure she keeps her hair short. Bring her out only in times of drought.

THE NYMPHOMANIAC

One of the biggest phallicies is that women do not enjoy sex as much as men. They most certainly do, only not always with you. All women are born Nymphomaniacs. However, the uncontrollable desire to mate with men slender of hip and fat of wallet does not manifest itself to the same degree in each woman. Far more than boys, girls are told from an early age not to do handstands while wearing skirts. But there is always one in every class who deliberately defies convention and brashly hoiks up her skirt and goes on to do cartwheels, the high jump and sometimes even the pole vault. It is not until every boy in the grade is following her about, slack-jawed and flushed, that she realises just how much power she wields. But, bless her, instead of going into politics, she goes into oestrus.

A lot of potential Nymphomaniacs were left sexually repressed as a result of the handstands and dresses indoctrination. They were led to believe from a young age that boys were little more than sex-crazed beasts whose depravity knows no limits, and this scared the pants on them for the rest of their lives. Quite tragic, really.

There has been a strange and subtle paradigm shift (this is the first and last time I will ever use these words in such close proximity to one another) in the way that social interaction is conducted in bars, sports clubs, gynaecologist's waiting rooms and other places where men know that women gather in large numbers. In the old days (1995–2002), a man would home in on a woman with the prospect of his own sexual gratification uppermost in his mind. Now, however, he has been bombarded with so much information about Female Desire Disorder that he thinks long and hard before approaching anyone for fear that she will react like a woolly mammoth that has been trapped in pack ice for the last three thousand years.

The peculiar thing is, even though a surprising number of men (93.9%) fantasise about having a Nymphomaniac fall in love with them, most would not be able to deal with the situation should it arise. When it comes to pace, style and strategy, men want to dominate and dictate. In short, they are domineering dictators with predatory instincts. So, when they are confronted by a woman who, the moment the bedroom door closes, turns into a voracious sexual beast capable of communicating only by grunting and moaning, they quickly lose their alpha maleness, which is so essential to a healthy erection ... I mean, relationship. The situation is not improved when she talks him into a pair of rubber handcuffs and then swallows the key. It is round about now that he realises she is suffering from a deep psychological disorder and has begun displaying symptoms unrelated to a fun-filled evening of chilled champagne and playful sex.

But let it be said that Nymphos are not sluts, nor are they hookers, although they might well be if they stopped shrieking and whooping long enough to realise how much money they could make from their disorder.

Step 4 – The first date

Congratulations. You have isolated your type and matched the right words with the right woman. No blood has been shed and, as far as you know, nobody is after you. The spontaneous chat went splendidly. You even walked her to her car when she left with her friends. And you told her that you want to see her again. At this point, there is not much else you can say apart from: "I'd really like to see you again." However, this is a stupid thing to say. You have consumed seventeen beers and twelve shots and should not be saying anything at all. The mere fact that she is still talking to you is a miracle in itself.

The concept of dating has different connotations for different generations. For instance, if you are nine and the girl you have your eye on is seven, you are fairly limited in your options. You could take her for a walk, but it only takes around fifty-three seconds to circumnavigate the playground and there is not terribly much you can accomplish in that time. Later in life, yes. But not when you are nine.

When you reach fifteen, you might be lucky enough to have parents who allow you to date. As you walk out the door with Julie tugging at her training bra, good old dad will say, with a twinkle in his eye: "No hitting beyond first base, son!" This is good news. When dad was fifteen, first base meant holding hands at the movies. He has no idea that first base has been upgraded to include free-range tongues and fingers. But this is not a book for kids. The dirty-minded little bastards have access to filth of their own kind.

Bryan, a straight friend of a gay nephew of my neighbour's neighbour's uncle, told me that he always takes his first dates to a restaurant. He said that next to soaking in a hot bath, women love to eat most of all. He said they are very like cats in that way. When I pointed out that cats hate water, he said that some of them love it. I asked him which ones, and he described some kind of animal that sounded like a cross between a Mexican Hairless and a Pygmy Rhinoceros. I challenged him to prove that this animal even existed, and he became defensive and quite hysterical. I ended up slapping him repeatedly just to calm him down. And also, I suppose, to punish him a little for making up such an outrageous story.

Where was I? Ah, yes. Restaurants. In my view, not an ideal venue for a first date. Eating is an intensely private affair and should be done either in complete isolation or with someone you have known for at least five years.

When it comes to feeding time, men are dogs by nature, while women are more like cheetahs. Teeth are bared at times like these, and you only have to watch your dog or cat to know that you don't hang about when the fangs come out. Although most of us have learnt not to growl and hiss while we eat, all we have really done is internalise these basic instincts. Apart from the more obvious hazards, such as ordering red wine with white meat or pink gin with green salad or blue sambuca with yellow rice, not to mention the old spinach in the teeth and spaghetti behind the ear, there are other dangers that lurk latently.

There are some men (me, for one) who cannot abide it when their dining partner starts feeding from their plate. It's cute and romantic the first time it happens, but when she finishes her food and then starts on yours on the pretext of wanting to taste a little of everything, that's when I want to plunge my fork into her eye socket, pluck out her eyeball and say: "Chew on this you greedy pig."

Then there's the matter of the bill. Way back in the olden days (2003), a man could quite confidently reach for the bill and with a manly flourish slap down his credit card or a wad of crisp notes while his date looked demurely the other way. It was to be expected. The man would pay. Not because he hoped for a quick poke on the first date, but because he earned more and it was the right thing to do. Happily, those days are gone. Women no longer expect men to pay the bill. Well, some do. Mainly the feminists, oddly enough. They have not, however, progressed to the point where they offer to cover the bill. Probably because feminism doesn't pay very well. At most, they insist on paying half. But more often than not, they snatch the bill away and perform lightning-fast calculations in their heads in the apparent belief that the entire (male) management is conspiring to overcharge her. You would be surprised at the number of times that they are right. But what many women fail to realise is that after a long, cosy meal by candlelight, few men want to feel as if they are a member of the Scorpions on a late-night forensic audit. And, if she does find that an extra coffee has been added to the bill, my advice is to excuse yourself and walk rapidly to the toilets. Hide there until the screaming stops. For the next few hours, you will be hearing a lot about "the principle of the thing".

Forget the restaurant. Go and play mini-golf on your first date. It's safer and a lot cheaper. And you get to let her win, which will count heavily in your favour when it comes to the possibility of a little first-date action.

Step 5 – Getting to know her (biblical)

This is the reason you were interested in her in the first place. It wasn't her trendy hairdo or her sparkling eyes. Nor was it her smile or perfect teeth. In fact, it had nothing at all to do with anything above the shoulders, but everything to do with that tight pair of jeans and low-cut blouse. The way her buttocks moved when she walked to the bar. The way her nipples strained against the soft cotton fabric. The way the lasers picked out the belly ring. You wanted to tear her clothes off and ravage her right there on the spot. You were so consumed by images of her naked that you knocked your beer into your lap.

So you have got to know her fairly well and you've reached the critical next step. The chances are that your woman reached this stage a while back, but was too polite to mention it. Their mothers trained them not to make the first move. Like most men, you will have missed the signs that she is ready to take the plunge. Like most men, you find it hard to believe that any woman, let alone one as desirable as this, would voluntarily remove all her clothes and invite you on board. But since she has not yet brought it up (even though she has already stuck her tongue in your ear and accidentally grabbed your crotch while looking for her car keys), you can stand it no longer and have decided to take matters into your own hands.

Once you decide to go for the home run, you need to arrange a time and place. These two elements are crucial, and will lay the foundations for your sexual relationship with this woman. The place you choose to commit the act will not only send a powerful signal as to what kind of man you are, but it will also give your paramour a very good idea of just how committed you are to the relationship.

So, remember that by choosing to go all the way, you are tipping your hand in a very big way. You are also setting a standard by which all other acts of love with this woman will be compared. Do not be alarmed. The best you can hope for is erectile dysfunction. This means that you will have no performance anxiety the second time around (if there is a second time). You will already have been through the fires of hell, so how much worse can it get? Since she will be expecting the worst, there is no chance of disappointing her even further. But since she is giving you a second chance, the odds are that you have grown even closer, as couples do when they survive terrible things together, like World War II and erectile dysfunction. You will be more relaxed, and hey presto! Even a half-trunk would be an improvement on your pathetic debut performance.

What you do not want to do is perform like a Viagra-crazed stud on your first outing. This sets a dangerous precedent, which you will be hard-pressed to match, especially when you go around to her place for a sexy third date only to walk in and find her clipping her toenails, wearing a mud pack and watching Jerry Springer with the sound turned high.

At some point in the proceedings, she may look up at you, or down at you, and utter three words that can throw an unprepared man into the coldest of sweats and the bluest of funks. Deceptively innocent in their brevity, these words are: "I love you." If you find yourself in the sack for the first time and you have not yet exchanged these words with her, you should know that they could come at any time. Studies undertaken in a Congolese research facility have shown that the words "I love you" are uttered 82.5% more times in bed than anywhere else.

In a previous era (1972–2003), women would not go to bed with a man unless he had given the verbal assurance that he loved her. Apparently, this is no longer a precondition. Today's woman is quite happy to hop willy-nilly from bed to bed without so much as an "I like you." Well, not all of them. An estimated 53.8% of all women will not drop their knickers until they hear those magic words. This percentage may not sound particularly high, but if you spend most of your formative years playing in the wrong half, life can begin to seem terribly unfair.

Stewie, a born-again anarchist who once went out with a beauty queen from Clocolan, told me that when he was younger he went to bed with a girl he had been dating for a few weeks. He was kissing her feet and trying to tear the condom's foil wrapping off at the same time just as she said it. Stewie said he froze. He said he had no idea where it came from, but that it rocked him to the core. Her words floated like three little parachutes drifting slowly towards a minefield. Every man knows that there is only one way to respond to these words in this situation. Repeat them, and add "too". And yet, Stewie was unable to do it. He claimed it was because he was an anarchist and therefore more ethical than most. Perhaps. I spoke to a lawyer friend about this, and he said the right thing to do would have been to lie to her. Just say it. Just say: "I love you too," and get down to the business at hand. But Stewie was trapped in a terrible place. Naked and unable to lie, he stayed perfectly still, the half-unwrapped condom still clutched between his trembling fingers. The seconds went by as if they were years. It was like a tennis match where the ball suddenly becomes suspended above the net. What to do? Whose shot is it? Stewie was one of the lucky ones. She eventually broke the terrible silence and said: "Is it on yet?" Later he thought she might have said, "Is it in yet?" and he stopped seeing her shortly afterwards.

The point is that reprieves like these are the exception rather than the rule. Women who use the words "love", "I" and "you" in the same sentence do not do so lightly. They expect an answer, even if it is a long rambling one that veers off into existential metaphysics, which is really the only place to go when you find that you cannot respond in the manner expected.

To cut things short, if you want her to fall in love with you, give her an orgasm. Use whatever it takes. Fingers, tongue, prosthetic limbs, vegetables, kitchen utensils, military hardware. Anything. Unfortunately, I am unable to explain in more graphic detail how to accomplish this feat because this is not that kind of book. You will have to check the Cookery section of your bookshop if you want more information.

Step 6 – Meeting her friends

Girls in their twenties come with the standard set of eight friends. One is her best friend who knows absolutely everything about her. Five she regularly bumps into and shrieks: "Oh … my god! I haven't seen you in ages! We must catch up!" The other two are overweight gays with self-image problems, but who are always up for a bit of shopping and a good old-fashioned gossip.

If her best friend doesn't have a love interest of her own,

you are going to be perceived as some kind of weird threat. Girls use emotional superglue when they bond, so when one gets a boyfriend before the other, there is always a certain amount of blood on the floor. When the best friend realises that she no longer has instant and unlimited access to her old buddy, she will begin to display symptoms ranging from mild jealousy and tears shed in private, to full-blown grief and at least one incident in a crowded mall that will leave you mortified.

Encourage your girl to exaggerate your good points whenever she is with her best friend. This should go some way towards dispelling her image of you as a worthless opportunist who is After One Thing Only. However, what sometimes happens is that your girl gets carried away and gushes endlessly about your prowess in bed, the one area in which the best friend cannot compete. Well, not without having a strapadictomy first.

Sooner or later, your girl has to leave town for a team-building weekend. "Take Angie to a movie while I'm gone. Aw, c'mon! Please? You two need to bond."

So when your girl returns on Sunday evening, she is understandably upset to discover two burly men from the fire department stamping out the last of the flames caused by such enthusiastic bonding that the sofa spontaneously combusted.

Remember that her friends are important to her, so avoid lisping loudly and flouncing dramatically about the room when she mentions that Brucie's nervous disorder is getting worse. I am not quite sure why women enjoy having gay friends. None of the men I know are remotely interested in having a bunch of bull dykes around for a game of poker. I think, in the case of women, it might have something to do with being able to talk to a man without him wanting to whip out his willy within the first five minutes of conversation.

Most women are heavily influenced by their friends. They can swing from Christian to Hindu, from conservative to liberal, from feminist to fuck-bunny, all on the word of a best friend. Most women who fall in love are blind to the faults of their man. The problem is, every time she gets together with her best friend, said friend grabs your girl by the shoulders and shakes her and says: "But, Janet, don't you see? He has the backbone of a jellyfish! He only wants you for your money/hamster/beach house/car!"

Throughout history, women united have been able to accomplish extraordinary things. Like winning the right to vote and … ah, well, that's all I can think of right now. But when the lone woman speaks, her voice achieves very little. At most, it might induce a headache in whoever is listening to her, but that's about it. Keep it that way.

Step 7 – Meeting her family

If you thought her friends were an ordeal, her family will be the ultimate make-or-break test of your relationship. A great poet once said: "They fuck you up, your mum and dad." Over the years I have often referred to these deeply insightful words to rationalise the aberrant behaviour of women I have known and loved.

Even though you and your girl might not have been together for long, you will have noticed one or two unusual quirks in her behaviour. We all have them to different degrees. Someone like my good friend, Ted Kaczynski, has quirks that are more pronounced than those found in most people. This does not make him a bad person and I, for one, think that three life terms in a Colorado jail is a little extreme.

But whatever odd mannerisms or strange behaviour you detect in your girl, know one thing: It is all a direct consequence of her upbringing. However, when meeting her father for the first time, it is best to resist the temptation to go up to him and say: "So you're the sick son of a bitch ..." Instead, pretend to treat him with deference and respect. Concentrate on working out the weak links in his psychological armour. Analyse his speech patterns and get to know his thought processes. This will make it easier for you when it comes time to analyse his assets and get to know his tax dodges. Remember, it is not only his daughter you are after; it is also his money. Unfortunately, he knows this long before he even gets to meet you.

Mom: "Honey, Jenny's bringing her new boyfriend around tonight."

Dad: "Quick, put on this old sack and roll up the Persians."

There was a time when the only thing a father had to worry about was his daughter coming home deflowered.

Now, they are far more concerned that the callow little bastard has his sights set squarely on the family fortune. The deflowering is bound to happen sooner or later, and all those expensive horse-riding lessons have probably taken care of that department, anyway. Today's father has a way of rationalising things when it comes to weighing up the pros and cons of his daughter losing her virginity or him losing his money.

So, right from the start, be aware that her father will be watching very closely for any signs of ulterior motives. Do not make the mistake of wandering through the lounge picking up works of art and holding them up to the light. I've only ever heard of this working once. When Rodney, a former employee of a friend's ex-boss, met his girlfriend's parents for the first time, he excused himself and went to the bathroom. Her father, on his way to switch the good whisky for a bottle of the cheap stuff, found Rodney in his bedroom on his knees with a jeweller's eyepiece screwed into his right socket scrutinising some or other bauble he had bought his wife for Christmas. Rodney couldn't think of a proper excuse quickly enough, so he said he was an undercover agent attached to the military wing of De Beers and was on a top-secret assignment to track down blood diamonds that had been secretly sold by the Sierra Leonean junta to a Swiss cartel of illicit gem dealers operating as a money-laundering front to fund George Bush's war on terror. To his eternal surprise, the father turned the colour of old newspaper and said he was welcome to keep the jewellery and his daughter for as long as he wished.

It is always a good idea to flirt with the mother. Not in front of her daughter, of course. And certainly never in front of her husband. But you can be sure of one thing: Mom hasn't been flirted with in years, and you are the first young buck to walk into the house since the gardener was fired. When nobody else can hear you, tell her that when you first saw her, you thought she was the sister. They love that. It doesn't even matter if your girl does not actually have a sister. It has been so long since Mom received a compliment that she will be like butter in your hands after that. Make sure you wipe your hands afterwards, because Dad can recognise Mom's butter from a mile off.

Unless Mom is a battered spouse, the odds are that she holds considerable sway when it comes to family opinion. So, when you leave after meeting them for the first time, there will be a family conference where everyone gets together to discuss your suitability in much the same way that great white sharks get together with baby Cape fur seals to discuss the sustainable utilisation of marine resources. But Mom's opinion will carry the day. If you have done your homework, Mom will be on your side. And even if Dad is dead set against you having anything more to do with their daughter, Mom will sit on her power base until he relents. I guarantee it.

Step 8 – Moving in together

Now that you have been dating for a while, it is likely that you will have come to several realisations. Among them, you will have realised that you want regular and immediate access to your partner's body. You have given a great deal of thought to ways of achieving this without giving her the impression that you are open to the possibility of marriage.

Living together is the obvious solution. However, it must be said that most women see cohabitation as the final pitstop on the race to the pulpit, so be very careful when introducing the idea of sharing a place. Base your suggestion on financial considerations. Tell her that since you spend so much time at her place, it doesn't make sense for you to keep paying rent on your place. She will get the message soon enough. Then you will discover that her place is way too small for both of you, and before you know it you will be spending your Sundays with a whole bunch of other hermit crabs scuttling about looking for the cheapest shell available.

It is important that you know from the outset that your participation is not strictly required in this process. All you really need to do is trail around behind the estate agent mumbling and nodding and occasionally tapping on the walls. At some point, your girlfriend will say to you: "What do you think, sweetheart?" Your answer may as well be: "I think Hegel was wrong when he said that the history of the world is none other than the progress of the consciousness of freedom" for all the good it will do. It is utter foolishness to try to convince a woman to live in a place where she doesn't want to live. While you are working out where to put the couch so that you can lie down and still have a clear view of the television and that little corner of ocean, she is standing in the bedroom like a human antenna picking up the vibrations of every other person who has ever slept in that room. Never mind the aesthetically pleasing flow from the kitchen to the lounge, or the cosy nook that would be perfect for your study. If she starts saying things like: "Something doesn't feel right," you should leave at once and never talk of that place again.

Look, if you really want to live there, you could try putting peanut butter on her arms and legs. Keep the door locked for a couple of days, and by the time she has finished licking it off, there is a fairly good chance that she won't stray.

Once you are living together, you have certain responsibilities and obligations as a common-law "spouse". However, these are overridden by your constitutional right to drop whatever you are doing and leave a hastily scrawled note on the fridge saying that you are going to Mexico and will probably never see her again.

There are some self-help books that say this is precisely the reason why couples should get married and not live together. They say cohabiting makes it too easy to leave. Well, *duh!* Isn't that the reason you do it in the first place? Do not, under any circumstances, listen to anyone who tells you that the only way a couple can share their lives is through the commitment of marriage. This, they will tell you, takes a lot of hard work. Don't you get enough of that from Monday to Friday? If you find you are having to work at your relationship, end it quickly and move on to one that doesn't take any work at all. Get out before she uses those four terrifying words: "We have to talk."

But don't be too hasty. Living together takes an enormous amount of adjustment, most of it from your side. For the first few days, maybe even weeks, she will pick up your clothes and towels off the floor and wrap her arms around you and say cute things like: "You're such a little piggy, but I love you anyway." This innocuous little remark is so overloaded with sub-text that if it was a taxi it would be pulled over and impounded. If you don't get the message, do not be surprised when you, the same cute little piggy of a month ago, somehow inexplicably turn into a giant boar with rank breath, bloodshot eyes and strings of glistening drool hanging from its unshaven jowls. And once she starts to see you as little more than a semi-articulate warthog, there is nothing you can do but pack your things and leave quietly.

While you were dating, she seemed to find your bachelor ways eccentric and endearing. But living together, these very same habits quickly become disgusting and abhorrent. It makes no sense, but there it is. It happens. So, if you like her enough to continue living with her, pick up after yourself, wash the dishes regularly, shave on weekends, pretend to like her music, stop drinking excessively, don't bring hookers home and, more importantly, put the toilet seat down when you are done. In return, you get to play with her hamster as often as you like. However, "often" is one of those words that take on a strange elasticity when applied to coitus.

Nearville, a former Jehovah's Witness once married to Clarissa, an American stunt double, said that when they first moved in together they were like a pair of rats from the Pfizer laboratory. Not even fire alarms or police raids could stop them. Then, he said, a light inside Clarissa seemed to switch off. Nearville said it was a bit like a fridge light in that you never actually see it go off, but you know that once you close the door the inside of the fridge is plunged into cold darkness. Women are very much like fridges, he said. The last I heard, Nearville was living with a middle-aged Catholic lay preacher called Steven.

The upshot is that living together can be a lot of fun, but don't expect your old pal Fellatio to come around as often as he used to.

Step 9 – Your first fight

Studies have shown that alcohol is a valuable and yet hugely underrated catalyst in opening up channels of communication between couples who have grown apart. Do not be afraid to use it. At the same time, try to avoid drinking and fighting simultaneously. I have seen many a fine carpet ruined by mock charges and spontaneous arm-flailing. If you want to give her a piece of your mind, or any other part of your body for that matter, put your drink down first. Keep one eye on it at all times. I have known women who can, through an incredibly fast sleight of hand, faster than the male eye can see, make a tumbler of whisky disappear and reappear days later covered in ants at the bottom of the garden. Keep the other eye on your adversary. Even though you have agreed only to fight with words of many syllables, women are duplicitous in times of emotional stress. Fight with her at the wrong time of the month, and the next thing you know the VCR is cartwheeling through the air in slow motion. An unexpected homicide tends to spoil the mood and should be avoided if possible.

It is also important that you and your partner match your drinks. In other words, if you are planning a fight, it will do no good for you to be guzzling cheap brandy while she sips on a glass of watered-down white wine. Either you both go lite or you both go heavy. Drunk people hate arguing with sober people just as much as sober people hate arguing with drunk people. And it does no good for both of you to be sober, either, because in this situation women have a 99% strike rate.

After a bout of domestic insurgency, it is always advisable to get straight into make-up sex. If nobody has won the argument, race each other to orgasm. You might want to spice things up by putting a little money on it.

Step 10 – Her first lesbian affair (it's not about the dyke)

Studies undertaken by a little-known Colombian cartel have shown that your beloved is going to have, or already has had, a rude experience with another woman. Your first instinct will be rage. You will then move quickly through denial, bargaining and threatening until you reach the final stage, which involves you spending long hours with your head in your hands wondering how you can get in on the action without coming across as an out-and-out degenerate pervert.

Heterosexual women stray for many reasons, none of which men are capable of grasping. While I appreciate that the penis is an unlovely animal at the best of times, it still remains one of the single biggest reasons for women to be attracted to men.

Research done by the North Koreans to counter what they described as imperialist Japanese propaganda, demonstrates conclusively that men would want nothing to do with women if they did not come equipped with such accommodating bits and pieces. I can only assume the reverse applies equally. None of which helps to explain why your girl's eyes have glazed over while she watches two topless Swedish backpackers rubbing one another with suntan oil at the municipal swimming pool. The naked female form is a beautiful sight to behold. Unless, of course, it is covered in yellow bruises, gelatinous rolls of blubber and clumps of spiky black hair. So I can understand why women would find other women sexually attractive. Their bodies are far more appealing than ours. Well, mine, anyway.

The important thing is to relax. The odds are that your girl is merely dabbling. She is, in professional terms, a Lipstick Lesbian. Her fling will probably not last, but while it does there is a very good chance that you will meet her partner in crime. It is very likely that this one is the genuine article. Like all predators, real lesbians love fresh meat. But even though you may feel resentment and jealousy bubbling to the surface, it is vital that you remain calm and not let on that you know what is going on. It's not about the dyke. It's about your girl getting something out of her system, whether she is satisfying plain old curiosity or something a little more primal. Either way, let her ride it out.

Step 11 – Your first affair

There is no point in you shaking your head and thinking: "An affair? Me? Never, as long as I live, so help me ..." Be honest, now. Before you could even finish the sentence your eyes had strayed from the page and onto the passing buttocks of a fine young thing. This is quite natural. When deciding to have your first affair, there are certain vital factors to take into consideration. First of all, is there enough petrol in the car? The last thing you want to happen is that you run out of juice as you leave her place. So, before embarking on an affair, make sure the tank is full. Some researchers, mainly from the former Eastern bloc, take the line that your motivation is important when choosing whether or not to be unfaithful to your partner. This is absolutely not true and provides a clear indication of why communism was such an abysmal failure in that part of the world.

A surprising number of men (100%) regularly think about having sex with women other than the ones they are with. Strangely enough, only 10.4% ever act on these thoughts. However, independent studies done in Malta have shown that men are congenital liars. And since men head most research teams, it is quite possible that this figure could in fact be as high as 78%.

It often happens that when a man decides to be unfaithful to his partner, it is not a decision at all. Per se. Rather, it is the decision of the brazen hussy who has been making moon eyes at him for the last month. Men do not enter into affairs lightly. For a start, they are easily confused. There is an awful lot to remember when pursuing an illicit liaison. Directions, dates, times, cover stories, deodorant. The list is endless. And, as I said earlier, or perhaps not, men are by nature indecisive when it comes to matters of the heart. They want a bit of this and a bit of that. And sometimes a little of the other thing, too. This is why it is invariably the woman with whom he is having the affair who ends up boiling the pet rabbit.

Ultimately, there is only one thing you have to worry

about when embarking on an extracurricular activity. That is getting caught. A former male supermodel I once met has the words "Never Underestimate The Power Of Denial" tattooed down his inner arm. At the time I thought this was a rather strange thing to do, but it makes perfect sense when applied to the pursuit of forbidden fruit. Never admit anything. If she comes home early and finds you and Brigitte rolling around on the carpet wearing nothing but World War II gas masks and each other's underwear, there is only one thing you can say: "Honey, it's not what it looks like."

Step 12 – The break-up

Break-ups can come in many guises: emotional, physical, psychological, financial and so on. However, for the purposes of this book, we shall deal strictly with the break-up of your relationship with the woman you first met and fell in love with several chapters ago.

Some poor fool once wrote a song with doomed lyrics about breaking up never being easy, but he was so wrong. Breaking up can be as much fun as courting. Maybe even more. However, studies undertaken in an uncontrolled environment by a group of Norwegian parapsychologists have shown that the dissolution of a relationship is frequently fraught with great trauma. However, it must be borne in mind that the sight of a man refusing to give up his seat for a woman on the

Stockholm to Göteborg train is enough to traumatise the average Nordic adult, male or female.

Breaking up need not be accompanied by pain and anguish. As the man, you should steer clear of such things. There will be more than enough gnashing of breasts and beating of teeth from the woman. You will need all the strength you can muster to go back out there and make the first move.

On the other hand, it is equally important to make sure that your break-up is not amicable. There are few sights more degrading than a man and his ex sitting at the Mugg & Bean sharing a couple of skinny decaf cappuccinos with sweeteners. Anyway, this could well be a moot point, whatever that means. The chances are that she would rather stick red-hot crochet hooks into her eyeballs than share anything with you ever again. And that is the way it should be.

Here are some helpful hints on the different methods of breaking up.

THE FACE-TO-FACE METHOD

Popular among younger men who have not lived long enough to grasp the true import of the situation. They often fail to realise that women do not appreciate the "courageous and honest" approach nearly as much as they think. Yet, they insist on sitting the poor woman down and holding her hand while looking earnestly into her eyes and then breaking her heart. "It's the least she deserves," he says, blissfully oblivious to the scalding irony of his words. Apart from anything else, the Face-to-Face Method opens you up to physical violence. I have known women who, from a reclining position, can move with the speed of a striking cobra. If you insist on using this method to end your relationship, all I can suggest is that you dress like an ice hockey goalkeeper. She may, of course, simply shoot you in the stomach when you least expect it.

THE ELECTRONIC METHOD

No mess, no fuss. Popular among older men who have been slapped, headbutted, bitten and kneed in the groin more times than they care to remember. There is a school of thought that says it is unethical and immoral to break up with a woman via e-mail or SMS. I have no idea why. It is far safer for everyone concerned. The only inconvenience is having to change your number when she begins sending you death threats every hour on the hour. When ending it via a text message, keep it short. Something like: "Sorry bt cnt do ths hve a gr8 lfe xx." There is no need to get poetic or melodramatic. This is an ending, not a beginning.

THE TELEPHONE METHOD

There is really only one thing to remember when you call to dump her. Never use the line: "It's not you, sweetheart, it's me." This is like throwing a chunk of raw meat to a ravenous crocodile. She will slam the phone down and pursue you with all the enthusiasm of a sniffer dog pursuing a black man wearing a hemp suit. You may think that by saying these words she will back right off in the deluded belief that she is the normal one and you are the fucked-up sociopath. Well, she won't. She will move in for the kill. She will arrive on your doorstep and start banging on the door with a blunt instrument. When you eventually let her in to avoid a public disturbance charge, she will smash the first ornament she comes across and then begin shouting: "So what's wrong with you what the hell's wrong with you tell me tell me you bastard are you going to tell me what's wrong with you?" And from there it is just a matter of seconds before you are a whimpering, craven mess clutching at snatches of philosophy to justify your fictitious inability to function in the real world. Weep, if you have to, but get the hell out of there as fast as possible. Let her keep the apartment.

THE CUT 'N RUN METHOD

This is by far the least traumatic way of breaking up, especially if you are to blame for the collapse of the relationship. The method is quite simple in its execution. When you come home from work, make sure that you follow your normal routine, e.g. grab a beer, kick the cat, make for the couch.

When she starts nagging you to put the music out and turn the dog down, say that you are nipping out for a box of smokes, and stop only once you reach the lower slopes of Machu Picchu. The problem with this method is that she will come looking for you. Next to Revenge, women want Closure most of all. And they can't get it if you are not there.

CLOSURE

Most men are quite happy to get Closure by means of a last pangalang. But you should not be the one to suggest it. For women, Closure involves shedding bitter tears and asking a whole bunch of questions that have no answers. Sometimes she will try to hit you. The best thing you can do is to stand there with downcast eyes, shaking your head sadly from side to side while deflecting the blows. Do not say anything. Do not make any sudden movements. Quite a few women still subscribe to the more traditional values, and for them genuine Closure only comes once you are sprawled on the staircase with a shattered spinal column and two bullets in the back of the head.

If you are one of the lucky ones, however, you will be breaking up with a modern woman and she will be the one to suggest a last pangalang. Be cool. This is not normal sex, so forget the Lou Reed and the box of tricks. It is vital that you remain submissive. I find it helps to pretend that you are Dian Fossey and she is a silverback. However, you may wish to try something else.

The important thing is to remember that she is doing this so she never has to think of you again. At this point, you will realise that nothing makes any sense at all, and you are ready to begin the whole wonderful cycle all over again.

Good luck.

How to make a man fall in love with you

(without losing your sanity, sense of humour and virginity)

Introduction

At the mere mention of this topic, there are women out there who will snort and toss their heads, as some women are wont to do at times like these. They will say that apart from Robert Mugabe's gushing biography of Tony Blair, this would be the shortest text in the history of the written word.

If they had to write this chapter, this is what they would say: "First, find a man. Second, offer to buy him a beer. Third, make it clear that you are available for casual sex." This, they would say, is all it takes to get a man to fall in love with you.

What absolute nonsense. It is a far more complex process. Modern man (often found wearing a skirt) is no longer the unconscionable slut that he once was. These days, men are far more discriminating. Just as there are a growing number of beers to choose from, so are there more hybrids of women than ever before. Faced with this smorgasbord, men have become more selective. No longer can their hearts be stolen with the offer of fellatio and a toasted sandwich. Well, some can, but then this is hardly the type of man you want falling in love with you. Today's man wants to be satisfied on many different levels, and women can no longer get away with boiling an egg for supper and grooming just three square inches of her body every second week.

The good news for modern women is that hard cash frequently facilitates the manifestation of love. It is a bit like magic, in a way. Whoever it was that said money can't buy you love clearly did not have enough of it. I am not sure if any studies have been conducted, but I am willing to wager a small fortune that a rich woman can make a poor man do pretty much anything that she wants him to do. Anyone who reads the newspapers on a regular basis knows that when it comes to men, stupidity and poverty are the same slope-headed brothers born of the predictably incestuous marriage between that capricious bitch, Fate, and her fickle brother, Free Will.

If you are looking for a man to fall in love with you, but lack the confidence to say so out in the open, then it is quite acceptable to feign support for one or other progressive women's organisation. Just as long as you wear a short skirt and shave your legs. In the old days (1658–2003), men subconsciously placed feminists somewhere between dykes and ugly and wanted no truck with them. This is no longer the case. It is patently obvious that modern man (2004—) has been lulled into a false sense of security by a new breed of feminist who has learnt to mask her true intentions behind a plethora of false flags and red herrings. Back then, men could see feminists, or rather their hairy armpits, coming from a mile off. They wore their hardened hearts on their sleeves, which was really quite a silly thing to do considering that a man forewarned is a man forearmed. Needless to say, forewarned, forearmed men with foreskins were even better prepared. So the feminists went underground. They grew their hair long and flirted coyly with the men at the bar, giving no indication that they were even remotely affiliated to the power-crazed, tribalistic Sapphists monopolising the dance floor and guarding the jukebox.

It's a trap, of course. And modern man is walking right into it, grinning foolishly while wearing his underpants on his head and happily gobbling up the male potency pills that the new feminists leave lying around. Once modern man is thoroughly incapacitated by spontaneous erections and the blood has drained completely from his brain, they will make their move. Once the office blocks are empty and the streets are full of writhing, pleading, onanistic wrecks, they will walk up and gently prise modern man's hands from his genitals and take his keys away. Modern man needs to start growing his nails. One day they will be the only weapons left at his disposal.

The last word on the subject goes to my American pen pal, Theodore John Kaczynski. Some of you may remember him as the Unabomber, the name given to him by the fascist Republican-controlled media.

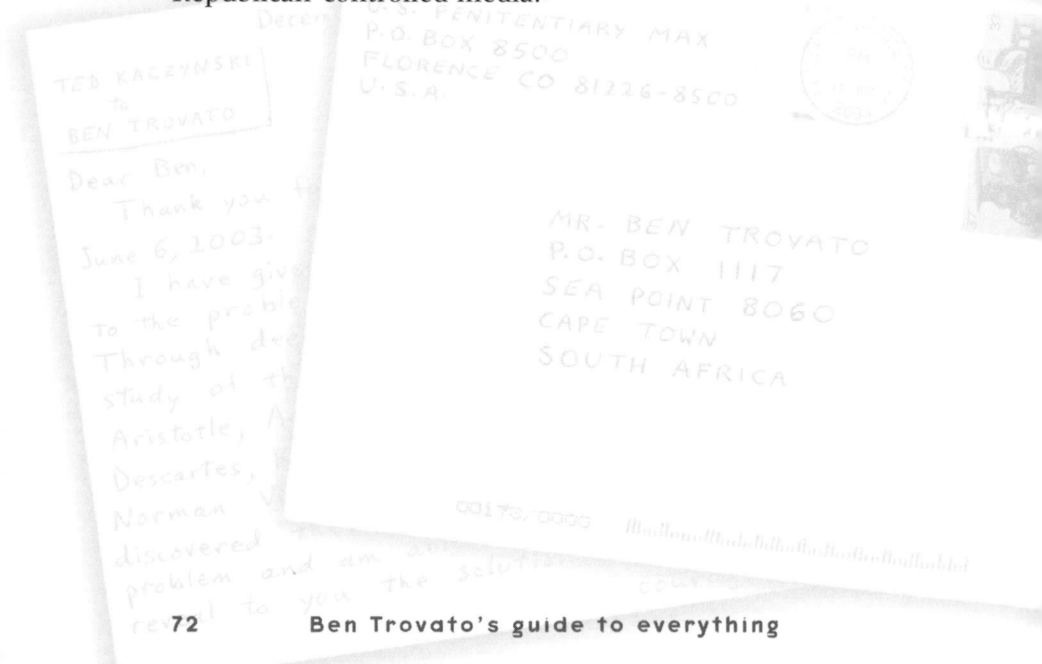

Dear Ben,

Thank you for your letter of June 6, 2003.

I have given much thought to the problem of Brenda. Through deep and prolonged study of the works of Aristotle, Aquinas, Leibnitz, Descartes, Kant, Hegel, and Norman Vincent Peale, I have discovered the root of the problem and am able to reveal to you the solution.

Brenda, whether she knows it or not, is a feminist.

Feminists are women who are dissatisfied with men but, because they have little insight into themselves, do not understand why they are dissatisfied.

What every woman wants is a Man, with a capital M. In other words, a man who has balls, not merely in the literal but also in the figurative sense.

In Western culture, a woman's ideal has traditionally been a "knight in shining armor". Of course, the knights of the Middle Ages were preeminently Men: courage was their watchword. That is why women have long yearned after them. But the knight in shining armor no longer exists in Europe. The samurai has disappeared from Japan. The fierce nomad no longer rides across the Eurasian steppe. No more does the African single-handedly slay a lion or an elephant with a spear. Nor does the American Indian drive the buffalo in a wild chase over the plains or creep silently upon his enemy to steal his horses or his scalp.

And who has replaced these true Men? Behold modern man (small m): He sits all day on his fat bottom, punching keys on a computer. Terrified of losing the "job" on which he is helplessly dependent, he cringes before his boss, invents petty subterfuges and little lies to conceal his errors and trivial misdeeds. Meanwhile his boss cringes before a bigger boss, who cringes in turn before a still bigger boss, and so on.

There are no true Men left; or rather, such true Men as

remain are in prison, for in the modern world it has been made a crime to stand up for oneself.

Is it any wonder that feminists have lost respect for men? Or that they resent men for failing to be the Men after whom (however vehemently they may deny it) their hearts yearn?

From the wisdom of the greatest philosophers, therefore, we may distill a solution to your problem: You must demonstrate unequivocally to Brenda that you are a Man, with a capital M.

In your first letter to me you voiced a suspicion that the reason why Brenda refused to have sex with you was that she had replaced you with one or two battery-operated devices – presumably, one or more vibrators. To prevent Brenda from using a vibrator, you must rigorously exclude all electricity from your home. First you must rip out all the electrical wiring. Then, whenever Brenda enters the house, you must force her to submit to a strict search to verify that she is not bringing in any batteries. Of course, Brenda will protest. She will have tantrums. She will scold, she will howl, she will rage. But you must remain firm. If you do so, all will be well: You will have proved to Brenda that you are a Man. She will love you passionately. She will *beg* you for sex.

On the other hand, if you fail to do as I say, then I can only advise Brenda to go up to the Ituri and see whether it is still possible to find a Mbuti who has single-handedly killed an elephant with a spear.

I feel inclined to wish you a merry Christmas and a happy New Year, but I will refrain. It would be a cruel mockery to wish a merry or a happy anything to a man who is stuck with a feminist for a wife.

Best regards,
Ted.

Some of you may find it hard to agree with the philosophy of a man serving three life terms for murder, but at least he can spell. This is a rare trait in any man, and my advice is that if a good speller ever crosses your path, grab him with both hands. Even if he does share a cell block with Charles Manson and Sirhan Sirhan.

Oh, dear (clutches head and sinks to knees), I feel a Disclaimer coming on.

I had every intention of seriously applying my mind to this section of the book and giving it the same attention to detail that I gave the previous section, but this no longer seems possible. My publisher is threatening me with legal action and I am only two weeks late with what they laughingly refer to as "the manuscript". The publishing industry has certainly changed. There was a time, not all that long ago, that writers would only be published on condition that they died first. Do me a favour. I have other things written into my contract. My publisher uses words like "Delivery Date" as if I was some kind of cud-chewing word-spewing robo-cow instead of the sensitive artist that I really am.

As loathe as I am to do it, I have to set aside my good intentions and comply with an archaic and restrictive piece of Roman-Dutch law. Frightening, I know, but when it comes time to firebomb the city, you will know where to start.

Let me begin before the Deadline Police kick my door down.

Part 1 Section A

Women have an appalling track record when it comes to making the first move. Ask any man what is the single biggest failing of women, and he will say: "Oh, that's easy. Their reluctance to make the first move." There are a few who will say: "Their reluctance to use the rear-view mirror for anything but pouting and preening and not watching out for people like me just because I'm on a goddamn motorcycle she thinks I don't exist," but we shall not be bothered with this sexist minority.

Right now in bars and clubs around the world, men of all shapes and colours are being roundly ignored by women who are stuck in some ancient mindset that says men should make the first move. I think it is important that somebody be blamed for this state of affairs. I asked Brenda who she thought was responsible, and she said men. "Excuse me," I said. "Men? Are you mad?" Brenda snorted and tossed her head. I eyed her apprehensively but she stopped short of pawing the tiles. "Who do you think came up with words like slut, floozy, harlot, tart?"

"The French?" I asked hopefully.

"Men. That's who," spat Brenda.

After making her clean up the spit, I got her into a friendly half-nelson and tried to make her understand that men no longer carry around gunny sacks full of nasty labels reserved for girls who come across as over-friendly or too forward.

In the days of yore (1987–1996), men were very different

from the men of today. They were Men, as Ted Kaczynski would have it. They were the people in charge of Situations. Whether it was mounting a rescue operation after an airline disaster or mounting a fresh young filly straight off the farm, men always had a firm grasp on the matters at hand. In a relatively short period of time, however, a lot of men have begun realising that being in charge is highly overrated. The dilemma is obvious. How to effect a smooth transfer of power while retaining the illusion of being in control and yet relinquishing nasty side effects like obligation and accountability? No easy answers there.

Never in the history of Humankind have men been this confused. And my advice to women is simple: Exploit their vulnerability. Men are genetically programmed to bring down the weakest in the herd, and they have been doing this successfully for thousands of years. Now it is your turn. Men, everywhere, have their flanks exposed. Their defences are in disarray and their confidence is shattered. Line up, ladies. The first move is all yours.

Chapter 2 Verse 11

At some point, if you want him badly enough, you will have to engage him in conversation. Remember that compared to you, a man is considerably less impressed by the first words. A man will not remember what you are wearing when you come up to him in a bar or restaurant or on the beach or in the parking lot of the magistrate's court. Ask him to repeat your first words ten minutes after meeting you, and he will scratch his head (actually, it's more likely that he will scratch his crotch) and say: "Didn't I make the first move?"

And while a woman approached by a man will make lightning-fast calculations based on body language, clothing, facial hair and shoes to determine her response, a man will react on a far more visceral level by watching her face.

This is why it is so important for you to make sure your face is doing the right things when you go up to a man with the express intention of getting him to fall in love with you. A friend's niece on her mother's side, Sandy, was telling me the other day how she had sidled up to a bronzed slab of a man lying on the beach at Camps Bay and asked him for the time. She said he sat up and looked terribly guilty. He apologised profusely for not having the time, then he hung his head in shame and dug his toes into the sand. She tried to touch him lightly on the shoulder as a way of thanking him for his trouble, but he recoiled as if she was about to strike him. I tried to make light of it and said that he was obviously batting for the other side, but it is far more likely that Sandy was wearing her Scary Face when she spoke to him. Sandy thinks she may have forgotten to change her face after the incident with the Johannesburg driver. It is not for nothing that an ill-tempered female horse is known as a nag.

Men are extremely sensitive to what a woman's face is doing when it is pointed towards them. For centuries, men have been trying to fathom out "the look". The ability of a woman to use her eyebrows and the corners of her mouth in such an infinite number of combinations to express such an endless range of emotions remains one of the most enduring mysteries of evolution. In terms of guerrilla warfare, a woman's face is the tripwire and her voice the splinter grenade.

In fact, you need not even worry about matching your face to your words. Go up to a man in a bar and say: "You remind me of a lizard in a leather coat," but say it in a low purr with a mysterious smile and one eyebrow raised. Guaranteed, he will wag his tail and lick your hand.

Page 9 Psalm 24

Once he has swallowed your hook, all you have to do is reel him in. But do not dawdle, as the waters are full of meat-eaters who will try to nibble at your catch. Women find men with other women very attractive. It is almost as if by having a partner they acquire some kind of secret stamp of approval.

The first date is when you will start getting to know what type of man he is. A lot of men would prefer you to skip this part and go straight to bed. In the minds of modern men, courting is an outdated and expensively circuitous route to a destination that you are both likely to arrive at regardless of how much time and money is spent getting there. Unhappily for modern men, the minds of modern women have not developed along similar lines. They want the whole deal. Flowers (not from the garage), phone calls (plenty), late-night text messages (romantic), movies (sexy), more flowers (still not from the garage), dinner (expensive) and so on.

You may be one of those women with a less traditional approach, in which case skip this chapter and proceed straight to Sub-Section 23c. However, the odds are that you are a sloppy romantic. This is an essentially feminine trait, although more and more men can be found surreptitiously sniffing flowers and crying in the movies. Hopefully you will not want one of these men to fall in love with you. Believe me, it starts with the flowers and ends with the gold lamé bodysuit and feathered mask at the Green Point Pride Parade.

Book IV 2nd Floor

Determining where you go on your first date will largely be dictated by the type of man he is. Don't be influenced by your addiction to sucking on oysters and quaffing fine champagne. Let him decide on the restaurant. But before you get to this point, it is Important To Ascertain Certain Things about the man who will fall in love with you.

GENDER

You may think this is a no-brainer, but I can assure you that there is many a slip twixt gangplank and ship. I live in Cape Town, the African equivalent of San Francisco with fewer steep hills but just as many cross-dressing deviants and a whole pack of dangerous goat-like creatures that are taking over Table Mountain.

The stories I have heard are frightening. Lucy, a good-looking brunette friend of some guy with a beard that I met briefly on the corner of Main and Beach, was taken out on a first date by a tall, good-looking pastor with the eyes of a poet and the hands of a steelworker. Perfect, she thought, and she went on to have a romantic dinner where the sparkling conversation and fine wine flowed freely. By the time Lucy kissed him goodnight at her front door (she's very old-fashioned), she was well on her way to falling in love. That was until she accidentally brushed her hand across his crotch and there was nothing there. Nothing at all, she said, not even the slightest hint of convexity. In the absence of tumescence, Lucy fled into her building. I asked her if he was not perhaps possessed of a very small willy, as some Catholic men are, but she laughed harshly and said he was clearly a she out for a walk on the wild side. I have no reason not to believe her. So be careful. There's a lot of dog-collar fraud out there.

BREEDING

Women are more inclined towards genetic snobbery than men. They expect their males to have a certain pedigree. If they had the self-restraint of men, they would publicly feel our biceps and peel our lips back to check our teeth. Even women of dubious bloodlines look for men of good stock. It is all about wanting to have children that do not grow up into thieving, murdering bastards. South African women have a particularly low strike rate in this department.

RACE

There is so much interracial fraternisation going on these days that it is becoming increasingly difficult to gauge a man's race with any real certainty. I am not saying this is a good thing or a bad thing. It is just a thing. The waters have been further muddied by black people using skin-lighteners and white people using tanning beds. If you have met a man and you want to know which race he belongs to before you go on a first date, I suggest you pick a fight with him and then take some of his hair or skin from under your fingernails to a biologist and ask for a DNA test. This may be quite costly, but at least you will be spared the surprise of finding out that your first child is the colour of an Easter egg. Or even the Easter bunny, for that matter.

MARITAL STATUS

Another tricky area. It is not uncommon for men to slip their engagement or wedding rings into their pockets when they are out on the town. This is a despicable habit heavy with symbolism that far outweighs the simplicity of the act. And yet, why should you care? If this is the man who you want to fall in love with you, it doesn't matter how many wives he has. Deal with them later. But if you were brought up by jackals in the middle of the Kalahari Desert and are meeting men for the first time, you will probably be concerned about these things. In this case, check his finger for the telltale white band left by a freshly removed ring. But don't jump to conclusions. It may be that he is recently divorced. Ask him. Asking doesn't hurt. In this case, however, asking should hurt. Whatever he says, keep telling him that he is lying. If he really is married, it won't be long before he cracks under pressure and tells the truth. Even if he is not married, he will admit to lying about something else, if only to stop the questions. Now that you have broken him down, you can start building him up again. This time, according to your blueprint. However, it may be that you are simply toying with him. This is acceptable sport for a Friday night, but should not become a habit. Men can only take so much badgering before they go gay or go away.

RELIGION

Having counselled thousands of troubled couples over the past three weeks that I have been in the self-help business, I have to say that more and more women are looking for men who are completely without religion. They find it only gets in the way of good, guilt-free sex as God meant it to be. Damn. I promised myself that I wouldn't mention God in this book, and already it has happened twice. Funny, that.

CREED

I don't know what this means, but some people find it important. If you are one of them, I suggest you keep it to yourself. Nobody likes a smartarse.

NATIONALITY

This is only important if you discover that the man you have your eye on is an Afghan on the run from Guantanamo Bay. Even though you are drowning helplessly in his big brown eyes, you do not want your name on any list that is being circulated inside the Pentagon. Stay well clear of men who are more interested in your passport than your pussy.

SEXUAL ORIENTATION

You are looking for a well-rounded man who knows what he is and what he wants. You do not want someone who has never made it out of the psycho-anal stage of his development. Nor do you want someone who would rather watch television than watch you strip. Be careful of any man who remarks on your shoes and hums Black Sabbath's "Changes" ("I'm going through changes ...").

Stratum 4 Paragraph 702

You will also need to know what strain he is. Here is a helpful guide to the various basic food groups according to phylum and subgenus:

THE NEW AGE MAN

The New Age Man with his incense and sarongs and collection of wind chimes is the end result of seventy-five years of feminism. I don't care. Go ahead. Spit and curse and hurl the book across the room. You know that I am right. Feminism's sole achievement has been to make men believe that they should be more like women. Just as all the original feminists went on to become men. Most peculiar.

THE JOCK

If you want a narcissist to fall in love with you, then you are way beyond any kind of advice I could give you. Your best bet is a Cameroonian faith healer.

THE OEDIPUS WRECK

The first time you meet him, you will be swept away by his suave charm and cutting wit. He will want everything that you want. The house in the suburbs, the double garage, the 2.3 kids. You will think it is a match made in heaven. And it is, right up to the moment that you find him writhing naked on the bathroom floor clawing at his eyeballs in a fit of remorse after killing his father and having sex with his mother. Granted, this is the extreme version, but it is advisable to stay well clear of anyone with Greek ancestry. Pyotr, a Romanian sandal-maker I met on the island of Crete many years ago, had a theory that the reason why so many men are screwed up is because their mothers chose to have a natural birth. He said that boys were never meant to be squeezed from the very aperture that they spend most of their adult lives trying to get back into. Pyotr claimed that the only normal men he ever met were all born by Caesarean section. Romanians are peculiar people at the best of times, so there is a very good chance that Pyotr had it all wrong.

THE BADGER

Like his namesake in the animal kingdom, the Badger will follow you around making sure that you have everything you need. On paper, this sounds like a fine thing. However, the Badger tends to be over-solicitous to a point where you want to find a heavy object and introduce it repeatedly to the side of his head.

If you think you might be with a Badger, but need some sort of conclusive proof, all you have to do is invite him out on a date and get him to pick you up at 8 p.m. Make sure you open the door in your tracksuit top and a pair of old shorts. Feign surprise at the time and tell him you won't be a minute. Every five minutes, shout out: "Almost done!" A non-Badger will let you get away with this for an hour. A Badger will start on you within seven minutes. It will start with: "Sweetheart, don't want to rush you, but I booked for 8.30," and then progress steadily through: "Can I give you a hand?" to "What the hell are you doing in there?" to "Right, that's it. Find yourself another boyfriend!"

Another area in which Badgers feature prominently is sex. There is nothing that makes a man hound and harass a woman more than the prospect of whipping off her knickers. Badgers frequently lack the sensitivity to tell the difference between: "No, no", "no, maybe" and "no, yes". This means that if they think they have a chance of getting you nekkid, they will badger you relentlessly until you threaten them with physical violence or give in. Badgers prefer that you do both simultaneously.

THE MAVERICK

Also known as the Rebel, the Renegade or That Crazy Bastard, the Maverick frequently has an outwardly normal exterior. He might even hold down a decent job like train driver or neuropharmacologist. However, the chances are that when he is alone, he can be found flipping the dials and diddling the drugs.

The Maverick has a brain like a computer virus. He enjoys burrowing into political and social systems and eating away at them from the inside. Be careful what you say in front of him. Casually toss a phrase like "conventional wisdom" in his direction, and he is likely to snort and say something like: "Ha. Now there are two of the most ill-paired words ever spoken. Wisdom evolves. Convention skulks in the corner and broods. Wisdom turns somersaults and chases sunbeams. Convention drives a tank with a stupid little fish sticker on its bumper ..." At some point you will want to excuse yourself and go in search of something powerful to drink. Mavericks can be difficult to understand without some sort of artificial accelerant coursing through your veins. Do not pursue one if your dream lies behind a white picket fence. Or a boundary of any kind, for that matter. Do not even think about trying to change him.

PETER PAN

A team of expatriate Filipino research students living on Hawaii's big island has found that a surprising number of men (98.4%) are afflicted with Peter Pan syndrome. Although not contagious, it does seem to be a genetically inherited condition. In layman's terms, fathers pass it on to their sons, who in turn pass it on to their sons and so on, until a wife uses a blunt instrument to end the line.

I once met a woman in the advanced stages of trauma caused by PPS. We were talking about housekeeping, as one does with married women, when she said: "You know, it's not easy having three boys." Now, I knew for a fact that she only had two boys. At that very moment both of them were clinging to my legs like baby orang-utans, making it impossible for me to get to the fridge for another beer. "What do you mean?" I said. I was about to pry the brats loose with a red-hot braai fork when my friend ran into the room with his underpants on his head making a high-pitched chattering noise pretending to be some kind of superhero. His wife looked at me with dead eyes, leaving me in no doubt as to what she meant. I left quickly, stopping only at the traffic lights to let the children out.

There are many things that act as triggers for this condition. Watch out for:

- Sports shops
- Explosions
- Fire engines
- Hardware stores
- Anything that operates with a remote control
- Car shows
- Stunts (cars and bikes)
- Brothels

Famous Peter Pan personalities include Paul McCartney, Cliff Richard and, of course, Peter Pan himself. It goes without saying that boyish good looks tend to exacerbate the condition. The likes of Charles Bukowski and William Burroughs suffered from many afflictions, but I doubt that PPS was one of them.

Men suffering from PPS are generally harmless, and aggravate nobody but their wives and girlfriends. However, it sometimes happens that the condition takes a strange and savage twist and the victim turns into ...

PETER PANDEMONIUM

This is Peter Pan with a substance abuse problem. Like his more conventional cousin, he also refuses to grow up and act his age. However, what puts him in a league of his own is that, as he gets older, he actually increases his intake of drugs, alcohol, loud music and loose women.

Peter Pandemonium progressively becomes a hazard to himself and all those around him. He leaves a trail of destruction in his wake. But he also has the capacity to make a lot of people happy, almost all of them women. There is a certain kind of woman who falls for his devil-may-care attitude. Driven by a host of solid and liquid chemicals, this silver-tongued pitbull has the ability to talk his way into and out of almost anything. Later in life he begins to think that he is indestructible, having miraculously survived several nasty accidents involving mountain slopes, wild animals and fast-moving cars. Do not attempt to convince him otherwise. Even when his wife packs up the children and flees to another city, it only registers as a blip on his hedonistic screen. Let him grow old disgracefully.

THE BOTTY BANDIT

Homosexual men can be a lot of fun. Apparently. I have no idea if this is true or not. But there are women out there who will defend their gay friends to the death. You could be one of them, for all I know. Fine. That's your business. But a word of advice: Don't have them over to your place all at once. Whether you are with a Jock, a New Age Man or a Maverick, the odds are that he is not going to appreciate having his Sunday afternoons shattered by a house full of flouncing queens mixing strawberry daiquiris and regaling everyone with wildly exaggerated tales of their Saturday night sexual escapades.

Quite a few women are physically attracted to gay men. Straight men find this completely inexplicable, but when you consider that women always want what they can't have, it begins to make more sense. Besides, a lot of gay men have the kind of bodies that straight men dream of having. You know what I mean.

What sometimes happens is that a woman will join a gym with the sole intention of firming up her bank balance. She monopolises the Stairmaster because the machine is in the corner of the gym that overlooks the parking lot. From this vantage point, she can see exactly who is driving which car. It's not long before a black-eyed stranger with ripped abs, slashed pecs and torn jeans steps from his metallic blue

Z5 and strides confidently into the gym. Nine hours later she is shrieking and whooping and throwing away the family name in the hope of acquiring his. Nine months later she is weeping and cursing and throwing pieces of fricassée chicken at his head. "Why?" she is wailing. "Why didn't you tell me you were gay?" He looks suitably shamefaced, and having half of his dinner stuck to his forehead doesn't help at all. "I thought I might … I never … I can't …" His voice trails off and he walks off to the bedroom to pack his clothes, horribly conscious that his hips are swaying just a little too much.

So, have a Botty Bandit as a friend, if you must. But, and it doesn't matter how hunky or well-hung he is, don't ever try to marry one. It's bound to end in tears.

Volume 8 Catch 22

Now that you have your man codified and assigned and you know precisely what you are dealing with, it is time for the first date. Let him decide where to go. This will create the illusion that he is in charge, and will save you a lot of trouble further down the line. However, if you have had to do all the work up to this point, then you will probably have to set up the date as well. Take the initiative. Some men are slower than others, and you may well have landed yourself one of those indecisive types that find it almost impossible to take a decision without some kind of divine guidance. If you are one of those women, leave immediately and don't look back. I have seen relationships where nobody can take a decision and "I dunno … what do you think?" can only be taken so far before the entire shebang collapses in on itself.

There are many places you can take a man on a first date, but avoid taking him to the one place that he really wants to go: your place. Sooner or later someone will cough at the copy machine and you will think she said "slut", and you won't be able to stop yourself from gouging her eyes out with the office stapler. Instead, try going out to a place where other, more normal people might be gathering.

Restaurants are generally a safe bet. They also give you a valuable opportunity to see if he knows his wine and his way around the cutlery (see Breeding). He will also be watching you closely and, since you are hoping that he will have fallen in love with you by the time dessert arrives, it is best that you do not embarrass him with an epileptic fit after the first hit of wine.

Men are impressed by women who eat heartily. Unless, of course, you happen to be a big fat pig, in which case devouring plates of food can be decidedly unattractive. But tucking into your meal with relish will send a subliminal message that you have a healthy appetite for all things hedonistic.

If your meal arrives first, wait for his to arrive too before laying into it. Starting without him sends disturbing signals on all levels, although men are increasingly open to playing from a handicap.

When it comes to ordering something to drink, take your

cue from him. If he orders a beer, try to refrain from ordering a triple Mai Tai with two flaming Drambuies on the side. You will come across as high maintenance and maybe a little mad. Instead, have a beer with him. Even if you have to go and throw up afterwards, it will have been worth it. Half the battle will be won. But don't keep on ordering beers, even if he does. He will start picturing you with a *boep*, and once that happens you may as well put down your knife and fork and walk right out of there. However, you should at least try to keep up with his pace. No man wants to be ordering his seventh drink while the woman is still nursing her first white wine spritzer. It makes him feel like an alcoholic, and even if he is one, it is important to remember that alcoholics in particular resent being made to look like alcoholics simply because they can't stop drinking. So try to keep up without looking like a complete booze hound. Men have a curious respect for women who can hold their liquor without turning violent.

Don't hog the conversation. Even though most men prefer silence to conversation of any kind, this does not mean that they have nothing at all to say. Very few men are sparkling conversationalists, but most manage to hold their own if they are given enough time and alcohol.

Early on in the date, make gentle enquiries about his education. You do not want a situation arising where you say between mouthfuls: "So, do you think Noam Chomsky was right when he said children are born with an inherent knowledge of the structure of language?" only to be met with the response: “I don’t believe in gnomes.” If this does happen, try not to fall off your chair laughing. Men enjoy being made to feel stupid marginally less than they enjoy having their testicles crushed in a metalworker’s vice.

When it comes time to leave the restaurant, let him call for the bill. If you do it, there is always the chance that the waiter will hand it to you. You do not want the bill. But nor can you hand it to him without him asking for it. If he has not noticed that you have the bill, slide it very slowly across the table using a napkin as cover. Distract him and remove the napkin. He will spot the bill and start fumbling for his wallet. This is your cue to start fumbling with your bag. “No, no. I’ll get it,” he will say. “At least let me get half,” you will say. At this point, most men will insist that dinner is on them. Even if they have just blown half their monthly salary, most men do not have it in them to allow the woman to pay her share, let alone the entire bill. Like rape, this has nothing to do with money and everything to do with power. Indulge him. But don’t sleep with him yet. Unless you really want to.

Section 9 Pudendum 4

Paulo, a Brazilian kickboxer who goes out with my neighbour’s third cousin on his father’s side, said that he once had a girlfriend who was so bad in bed that he used their intimate moments together to work on his hip action for the next fight. He said she never seemed to notice, but I find that hard to believe.

A man will have sex standing up, sitting down, crouching, standing on his head, standing on your head, driving, in his sleep and in the middle of Christmas dinner. You only have to say the words: "Do you want to have …" and he will be on you like a cane rat on a baby dove.

Sex is about the most dangerous and intensely personal thing that two people can do together. That, and sharing the same bank account. But even though most men are aware of the emotional significance of an inaugural coupling, they do not award it the same level of importance that a woman does. While you are more likely to be worrying about whether you should be taking such a big step, he will be praying to all manner of gods that the dreaded attention deficit disorder does not strike him in the nether regions. He will also be worrying about the size of his willy, thanks to the endless articles in women's magazines telling him that there is nothing to worry about.

Manchester United 5 Real Madrid 0

Somebody once said you can judge a man by his friends. Plato, probably. Then again, Plato never had any friends, so what did he know? None of those Greek deviants had proper friends. They all slept with young boys and took mind-altering drugs.

Most men are heavily influenced by their friends. They are also heavily influenced by alcohol, but mainly by their friends. Their drinking buddies, actually. Their attitude towards you will be an indirect reflection of the attitude of his friends towards your relationship. I know it sounds twisted, but it's true. And it gets worse. Men who get together for a few beers and don't talk about women are either into computers or other men. You do not want to be involved with either category.

Remember that your man is still a snigelton in his mind. No, he is not. He is a singleton. I have no idea what a snigelton is. The first time he gets together with his mates after meeting you, he will not immediately tell them that he has met the most wonderful woman in the world. It is the way of the bachelor to bemoan the lack of suitable women, i.e. women who drop their knickers at the sound of a high-pitched whistle. He knows that admitting to having met you will break the sacred ring. So he buys everyone a few rounds and waits until everyone is plastered, and then he says: "I met someone the other night."

The others round on him as the senators rounded on Caesar. Some look in awe, others in horror. When you tell your friends that you've met someone, they are quite likely to say: "What's he like?" and "What does he do?" When he tells his friends he has met someone, they ask the same questions, but the difference is that they add "in bed" to the end of each.

A lot of single men spend a lot of their time getting laid vicariously. So, if you overhear your man telling his mates that when you are naked together it's like sharing a bed with a giant oil-coated squid, you should realise that he not only means this as a compliment, but that he is also feeding his bachelor buddies' fantasies to help get them through another week.

The quickest way to lose your man is by turning on his friends. Not turning them on. Turning on them. It is important that you make the distinction. Remember that he has known them a lot longer than he has known you. Having met you, his loyalties are now divided, and he is easily confused. Weaning him off years of Friday night debauchery with his mates will take some time. Don't force him to go the cold-turkey route. Right from the start of the relationship, you need to give him the impression that you don't mind if he goes out for a few beers with the old crew. But don't overplay your hand. Try to avoid encouraging him to go out for as long as he wants any night of the week. This will only make him suspicious. He will begin wondering about your ambivalence, and before long he will have convinced himself that the reason you want him out of the way is because you are having an affair with his best friend who, strangely enough, hasn't made the last two Friday night sessions. Then you will never get him out of the house. At the same time, you don't want to let him completely off the leash. I have found that men respond best when they are on one of those expandable leashes that gives them the impression that they can run free, but just as they reach the point of no return the leash runs out and they are yanked up short. This allows you to reel your man in without too much of a struggle. It's a bit like having a disorientated barbel on the end of your line.

If you reach a point where your man is still spending the same amount of time with his friends as when he was a bachelor, you may want to consider using the most powerful weapon in your arsenal to bring him to his senses. Don't be coy. You know exactly what I am talking about. However, it is important that you do not use your hamster as a weapon. Rather use it as bait. More fish have been caught with tasty morsels than with baseball bats. So, make it clear to him that if he goes out with his friends on a Saturday night, he should try to be home by midnight, otherwise you and your tasty morsel will be fast asleep and quite unavailable until late Thursday afternoon. Once he realises this, he will quickly rearrange his schedule to fit in with your hours of business. Women and booze are the fuel that feed every man's will to live, and he will soon enough adapt to circumstances once he realises that bottle stores are shut and legs are closed as a consequence of his actions.

Brides 7 Brothers 7

When he met your family, your mother batted her eyelids while your father went straight to his study and began oiling the Walther PPK. On meeting his family, you will find things turned around. His father will suck in his giant beer belly and try to make you laugh by indulging in a little horseplay with his son. His mother, on the other hand, will have you down as a cheap slut the moment you walk through the door. She may even be right. But it is more likely that she decided long ago that no woman would ever be good enough for her boy. Mothers like this worry me. What terrible things do they know about their gender that they aren't sharing with the rest of us? Do they have some unique and terrifying insight into the female psyche that, if made public, would destroy life as we know it? Perhaps it's not that complicated. Perhaps they are simply barking mad.

Version 9.2 Upgrade Mi-Rs

Statistics show that your first fight with him will be directly or indirectly linked to what you perceive as his inability to commit. When you are with your friends, you make light of the issue. You paint him as a devilish young rogue clinging to bachelorhood, and make out that all he needs are a few gentle nudges, or perhaps violent shoves, to get him to commit to a proper relationship with you. This is all rubbish. Men don't balk at commitment because they want to eat instant meals, talk to the cat and wear dirty underwear for the rest of their lives. They have trouble with commitment for one reason only, and that is because they are not in love. It really is that simple.

So, now that the secret is out, you might want to think twice before light-heartedly joking about his inability to commit. It follows, then, that picking a fight with him on the grounds of his inability to commit is futile. You may as well fight with him for not being in love with you. At least there will be some entertainment value in watching him trying to answer one of the world's great unanswerable questions.

Whatever your first fight is about, it is vital that you have sex immediately afterwards. If you are pressed for time, you can even make a start while you are still arguing. This is particularly effective if it looks like he is winning the argument. My personal team of Puerto Rican researchers found that seven out of ten couples stay together beyond the first year if they engage in sex during or after a fight. They also found that two out of five couples never survived their first month because they made the mistake of having sex before fighting. The post-coital male is dull-witted and slow moving, while the female is generally dissatisfied and irritable. This is not a good combination for an effective fight. Studies conducted by a rival team of researchers found that in seven out of eight cases, the man will lose an argument if he has it right after sex. Particularly if the argument is along the lines of:

She: "That was undoubtedly the worst sex I have ever had in my life."

He: "........"

Flat 24a Marine Drive 55

Men have a well-developed ability to suffer in silence. Born with an innate sense of guilt, they can tolerate endless emotional blackmail and sexual deprivation on the vague assumption that they probably deserve it.

Then, one day, a strange woman will toss a kind word his way, and he will begin trembling all over like a freshly whipped puppy. And if she happens to stroke him, he will go down on all fours and keep licking her feet until he hears commands like "roll over" and "give me your credit card".

Unfortunately for men, women have a 95.3% strike rate when it comes to detecting signs of an affair. This means that cheating men are left with just a 4.7% chance of weaselling their way out of the situation. When men lie, they lose all control of their eyes. They swivel randomly in their sockets to avoid focusing on the object of their deception. This does not go unnoticed, and the only reason the divorce rate is sky-high is because men cannot control their eyeballs when they lie.

Genesis 13 Robert Palmer 6

An unidentified team of researchers from Tajikistan recently released controversial new findings that demonstrate women to be as duplicitous as men when it comes to fiddling with the new violinist in the orchestra. However, their findings were widely discredited almost from the moment they became known. It seems that society is more comfortable with research done in civilised countries such as England and certain parts of North America.

There is broad agreement that men are genetically driven to spread their seed far and wide. Women, not having a spreadable seed, are inclined to stay at home knitting before the fire with the front door unlocked in the hope that a passing stranger will come in and do a spot of impromptu ploughing. This is all a pack of filthy lies. Women, just as much as men, want to be ravaged mercilessly on a regular basis. The only difference is that women expect the ravaging to be preceded by dinner and perhaps a movie, followed by a bit of a hug and a nice chat.

If you want to have an affair, don't give it a second thought. Even though, compared to men, you have a more developed sense of right and wrong, you are far better equipped to lie with a straight face. Watch those eyebrows, though. This balances things out nicely, and unless you are really careless, you should have many happy months, or even years, banging the butcher's son without being caught.

Mary 1 Lamb 0

What I find remarkable is that one out of every two marriages does not end in divorce. This speaks volumes about what kind of society we have created and I, for one, would think long and hard before bringing a child into a world where he runs the very real risk of being among the 50% that get stuck with the same person until he dies.

Everybody knows that beyond a certain point, every couple has to choose between love and sex. What happens is that the man chooses sex and the woman chooses love. Perfect. Now what? Neither of them have the energy or the inclination to start all over again with someone new, so they agree to stay together on the grounds of "companionship". I have never heard such crap in my life. If you want a companion, get a Labrador. They make ideal replacements for the obsolete husband, not least because they share the ability to drool, break wind and eat like pigs all at the same time.

When deciding to dump him, it is important to bear in mind that men are extremely sensitive to rejection. For men, rejection implies failure. And next to running out of beer, men fear failure more than anything else.

Women are nowhere near as badly affected because they have never been encouraged to succeed, so they live in a permanent state of failure. Except it is not called this, of course. I would rather not say what it is called, as there are certain unspoken male codes that cannot be violated. All I can say is that it somehow ties in with the cycles of the moon and an ancient primal urge to breed and shop.

I am not suggesting that, when contemplating cutting him loose, you should bear his ego in mind for fear of hurting him. The truth is that he needs to be hurt, for the sake of the species. Unlike women, men grow stronger with every crushing blow dealt to them by the opposite sex. Their scar tissue is made from titanium, while your scar tissue is porous like a colander. This allows fresh, untainted love to seep through. If your wounds had to be hermetically sealed, like the wounds of men, there is a very good chance that you might be disinclined to continue propagating the species. And what kind of world would that be? A world without people, a world populated only by trees and birds and animals, that's what kind of world it would be. Hmm.

Instead, I am suggesting that you treat his fragile ego carefully for no other reason than your personal safety and the safety of those around you. Men can only take so much rejection (13.4 ml per litre) before they snap. Luckily, men have access to a very broad range of snapping methods, the most harmful of which is the taking up of golf. There are women who call themselves "golf widows" long before they even get around to shooting the stupid bastard as he heads for the 19th hole for the 375th consecutive Saturday.

Anyway. We have both reached a point where we have to move on: you, to the beginning of the cycle, and me to the next section. I had intended to finish this madness right here and now, but then I thought how dare these publishing types restrict me to a certain number of words. I am the one who will decide when I am done. And I am not yet done. So, here is an entirely new section containing free advice to help you get through life.

Ben Trovato's guide to every-thing else

Getting the most out of a mid-life crisis

When I turned thirty, shortly after marrying Brenda, I suffered a spate of premature mid-life crises. It was terrible. The sweaty palms, blurred vision, projectile vomiting. I wouldn't wish it on my worst enemy. Then, just when I thought I would have to take my own life, a close friend pointed out that I had been drinking solidly for a month and that my body was probably rejecting the toxins. I found it hard to believe. After all, what is a mid-life crisis all about if not rejection? How could he be so sure that my body was reacting to the alcohol and not to my having committed an unnatural act by getting married so young when I still had so much to accomplish?

Now that I am older, I realise that he was right. I was simply in the throes of a multiple hangover. The real mid-life crisis is probably far worse. I'm just not sure that I will recognise it when it hits, but I am looking forward to getting the tattoo and belly ring.

How to make casual sex even more casual

For a start, lose the corduroy jacket. You might think it makes you look casual, but all it really does is make you look like a journalist. And nobody wants to be mistaken for one of them these days. Not even really desperate women will sleep with these harbingers of doom and peddlers of pessimism.

The best casual sex occurs when there is no verbal communication whatsoever between the parties concerned. Talking detracts from casual sex like nudists tripping on acid detract from holy mass. If you walk into a bar and spot a woman with whom you would like to have casual sex, wink at her several times and motion with your head towards the door. At the very worst, there is an outside chance that she will think you have Tourette's syndrome and go home with you out of sympathy.

Unfortunately, casual sex has been saddled with a bum rap in recent years. Thanks to a team of French researchers, casual sex is now synonymous with a lingering, painful death. Not much of a laugh in that. Trust the French to spoil everyone's fun. Bastards.

Surviving foetal alcohol syndrome

First, do not blame yourself. Second, keep your mouth closed when you are not talking. A gaping maw is a dead giveaway. Besides, drooling is unattractive and there are no excuses for having a lazy jaw. If you are unable to control your mandibles, have them wired shut. At the same time, you may want to consider giving up any ambitions of controlling the world. It is far bigger than your jaw, although fewer things live in it. Concentrate on the smaller issues. Like secretly putting increasing amounts of rat poison in your mother's cheap wine every night.

Once mom has passed on and you have spat on her grave,

try to control your urge to drink. If you find this difficult, then at least try not to mix your drinks. It is important to remember that you are genetically programmed to drink. Nobody will blame you. Well, some might. But don't let that stop you. Know that you are unique. People who watch rugby like to think they are one of you, but they are not. I know one of these impostors. His only claim is having a mother who got drunk and copulated with her brother's wife's husband. And that kind of behaviour is nothing uncommon in the gated communities that surround us today. So, I say rejoice in your dysfunction. Go out and make new friends. Just don't talk to them or try to make eye contact and you will be fine.

The truth about the Qur'an

Just kidding! Sheesh. Can't you guys take a joke?

How to be happy

Look, it's really not that difficult. If you are bipolar, take the blue pills. If you are not, take the yellow ones. Happiness is a chemically inspired condition. It is one of those cheap, overrated emotions that achieves nothing at all. Jealousy, on the other hand, is worth striving for. Jealousy has the capacity to inspire machete fights at dawn, which is a whole lot more exciting than watching someone walking about smiling and humming snatches of song. But if you want to experience a real emotion, skip Happiness and Jealousy and go straight to Fear. If you are one of those pathetic suburban lapdogs who are too afraid to go in search of something to terrify the life out of you, then you do not deserve to experience the king of emotions. Happiness, pah! It only leads to babies and polo-neck sweaters. And we have more than enough of both in this so-called world of ours.

How to behave when a homosexual gives you the lazy eye

This happens more often than you might expect, and how to react is fast becoming a question that regularly enters the mind of the heterosexual male, often at the most inopportune time. Jason, a friend of a friend's friend, told another friend who told me about a recent incident in which he was lying in a strange woman's bed waiting for her to emerge from the bathroom, where women on one-night stands disappear to for exactly six minutes before they reappear to ravage you so mercilessly that you would have forgotten their names had they bothered to introduce themselves to you in the first place. Jason said that thirty seconds before she was due to whip the bathroom door open, he spontaneously recalled an incident that had occurred two days previously. It's not like he was dwelling upon it. Or so he says. The incident involved a humdinger of a queen wilfully squeezing his buttocks while he was waiting for a mutton roti at an unnamed late-night curry den somewhere between Salt River and Observatory. Jason said the incident disturbed him less than it should have, but that it came back to haunt him at the worst possible moment. So when she emerged from the bathroom and flung herself at him, he was unable to muster the requirements. This, in turn, led him to begin questioning his sexuality. Actually, when I heard the story the first thing I thought was that Jason is one of those poor bastards who have half a millilitre too much oestrogen in their bodies without ever realising it.

I suppose there is nothing wrong with a little harmless flirtation. If a botty boy gives you the lazy eye, you could always give him one back. I have never done this myself, you understand. I am always very quick to avert my eyes, although this can also give the impression that you are being coy, so it is important to dart him another stern look before letting your gaze trail away to the nearest woman. However, homosexuals operate on a secret code of mixed signals, so there is a very good chance that you have just told him that you will meet him upstairs in the dark room in twenty minutes. If you accidentally catch his eye again and he is making flicking movements with his tongue, move quickly to the nearest woman (it need not be the same one) and stand as close as you can to her without arousing suspicion. If she says: "Fuck off, Batman" and moves away, you may want to try another bar.

How to deal with self-pity

Wallow in it. Wallow like a big fat warthog in a mud pool. Put on Nick Cave's *Murder Ballads* and take the elevator all the way to the basement. Do not stop at the ground floor. All the losers are on the ground floor. You are not a loser. Well, you are, but you are a different kind of loser. The ones huddled together on the ground floor lack the courage to indulge in pure 100% hi-octane self-pity. For a start, they are missi~g self-hatred, a vital component of remorse that only the true masters of self-pity are able to excavate from the tortured belly of this restless beast. Go all the way down. Take a deep breath and plummet. Put on *Songs of the Damned*, light a candle, pop a Seconal and take out all the old photos. After that, the only way out is up.

Surviving erectile dysfunction

This is a condition created by many different factors, chief among them the features editor of *Cosmopolitan* magazine. She created the condition so that she could reassure her readers that it is not their fault. *Cosmo* readers are damn near perfect, and if they are unable to get their men aroused, well, they should simply cancel their subscriptions and start reading *Farmer's Weekly*.

It is a little known fact that erectile dysfunction has nothing to do with men. It is not caused by the stress of closing yet another multi-million dollar deal. It is not caused by clogged arteries. It is caused by women. The ex-boyfriend of a former friend's girlfriend, Bobby, told me that he has never experienced erectile dysfunction while on his own. The only times he has ever had trouble with his willy were when women were in the area. Bobby is not bent. I have seen pictures and I can attest to that. Bobby is among countless men who frequently find themselves naked with women whose only appeal turns out to lie in the fact that they will have to leave sooner or later. Some say beer is to blame. Far be it for me to defend beer, but let me just say that while beer might be a contributing factor in taking the grunt home in the first place, it also serves as a self-defence mechanism in that it prevents you from acting on your misguided impulse. Beer is good in that way. I have never met a man who has gone home with a Charlize Theron lookalike after a few pints and said the next day that he couldn't get it up. The fact that I have never met a man who has gone home with a Charlize Theron lookalike is not the point. You know I am right.

So, men, do not feel shattered when you are stricken with erectile dysfunction. Do not be afraid to tell the truth. And you, women, shame on you. Shame on you for blaming the beer, the cigarettes, the stress, the volatile heart condition and the ex-girlfriend.

Erectile dysfunction is caused by women with yak breath, unshaven armpits and smelly crotches. It is caused by women who talk their way into your bed and then, when it is too late, you find they cannot spell. It is caused by women who lie through their teeth and kiss like Gila monsters.

How to get a job

First of all, make sure that you are not white. White is last year's black and is hopelessly out of vogue among the new elite. If you cannot afford a full-body skin graft, then be very humble when applying for a job. Keep your eyes on the floor and your hands where they can be seen.

How to keep a job

Everyone is always saying how, even though they are desperately unhappy at work, they still count themselves very lucky to have a job in these harsh times of financial belt-tightening and racial quotas. This is just plain stupid. There have been no fundamental changes in the workplace since the Industrial Revolution. All that has happened is that a bunch of backstreet businessmen and assorted capitalist lackeys have spawned a slew of books with titles like *The One Minute Manager* and *Six Secrets to Success*.

In turn, the hard-nosed but generally even-handed bosses of the past began devolving into the two-faced expatriate Eurotrash scumbags who run most companies today. Where they once ruled by respect, they now rule by fear.

Through the underhand corporate philosophies propagated by people like, well, let me rather not mention names, today's employers have learnt how to make their workers believe that they are lucky to have their jobs. If the propaganda has been installed correctly on the employee's internal drive, it doesn't matter how appalling the working conditions may be. The poor bastard could be using blunt nail scissors to cut matchsticks into equal lengths for eighteen hours a day, and if the boss has applied the proper techniques, the shattered employee will drag his numb brain and body into bed at night and thank God he has a job in these hard times.

The strategy to get a worker into this state of mind is not particularly sophisticated. In fact, much like poker and marriage, it is based on the art of bluffing.

This is how it works:

EMPLOYEE: "Sir, I've worked here for twenty-five years without a raise. But I'm not complaining. However, I'd like to have this Friday afternoon off."

EMPLOYER: "Well, you can't. And if you don't like it, you can leave. There are a thousand people lined up around the block waiting for your job."

EMPLOYEE (sobbing): "I'm sorry, sir! I don't know what came over me!"

If the employee had not allowed himself to have been so effectively brainwashed, he might have answered thus:

EMPLOYEE (letter-opener against employer's carotid artery): "You sick, twisted motherfucker. You don't scare me. Go ahead, do your worst."

Try it. You will be surprised at the results.

How to lose a job

See above.

Six habits of highly successful people

- Cocaine.
- Using the rear-view mirror to check for shnarf on upper lip while driving.
- Talking loudly in public.
- Driving slowly in the fast lane.
- Not listening when people are talking.
- Farting in the Jacuzzi.

How to analyse someone with the sole intention of getting laid

Rule number one: Never take a guess at their star sign. This is strictly for amateurs. When I was young and foolish, I did this on several occasions, but only because the women were always wearing something that suggested that they were astrologically inclined (dreamcatcher earrings, tie-dye pants, pierced tongue and so on). Without fail, the conversation went like this:

ME: "Hi." (Nod and smile.) "You're a Gemini, aren't you?"
HER: "Um, no."
ME: "Of course. Now I can see it. You're a cusp. Taurus, right?"
HER: "No." (Turns to friend and mouths "help".)

If you are going to try such tomfoolery, make damn sure you know your signs and what they mean. I have no idea, and yet there are still times that I feel inclined to use the line. I know for a fact that there are women out there who will sleep with any man capable of guessing their star sign, but while she may be fun for a while, it won't be long before you start considering how to short-circuit her electric yoga mat. You will wake up on Sunday mornings to the stench of cheap incense and the sound of the Tarot deck being shuffled. Believe me, there is nothing that ruins a lazy Sunday morning more than getting the Death card twice in a row. She will laugh gaily and tell you: "No! No! It's a good card!" It is not a good card. It has a picture of a skeleton on it. How good is that?

Where was I? Oh, yes. Psychoanalysis as a tool for achieving despicable ends. Psychoanalysis is easier to do than it is to spell. Of course, the experts won't tell you this. If their dirty little secret had to get out, nobody would bother wasting enormous amounts of time and money in stuffy little lecture rooms so that they could get a fancy-looking piece of paper saying "Psychoanalyst" in order to spend the rest of their lives in stuffy little offices talking to mad people.

The only real difference between the Trained Psychoanalyst and the Street Psychoanalyst is that the Trained Psychoanalyst nods a lot and gives the mad people useless bits of advice in return for huge sums of money, while the Street Psychoanalyst laughs a lot and gives mad people drugs so that he can have sex with them. Both can be found staking their turf on the moral low ground.

A lot of fun can be had with emotional disorders. Some

people seem to think that the disturbed mind is a thing to be treated with respect and caution. Nonsense! Embrace it! Just make sure that it is not carrying a flecking knife when it embraces you back. What makes street psychoanalysis such fun is that you can invite all your friends around to your place and hypnotise them, and then delve into their collective subconsciousness. If your friends are anything like mine, they are unlikely to be harbouring anything particularly interesting. Maybe a bath-time fondle from Aunt Julie or a glad-hand from Uncle Pervy, but nothing to write home about. So what you have to do is make up some really wild stuff once they come out of hypnosis. Tell them that they were recounting the most horrendous stories of abuse, committed both by and against them. They will be so disturbed by this revelation that they will come back to you over and over for advice and suggestions. This is when you start charging them or sleeping with them. But more on this fascinating subject later.

How to behave on the wine route

Most importantly, do not be intimidated. You will encounter people from the horsy set. In fact, some of them may even be horses. They let anything in on some of these estates. The wine route goes back hundreds of years to a time when black labourers would go from farm to farm begging to be allowed to work in return for a bottle of wine. This fine tradition continues today. The only difference is that the labourers are no longer allowed anywhere near the manor house. The wine is delivered to them in the fields.

While on your wine-tasting excursion, make liberal use of words such as "woody", "petulant" and "cheeky". These terms can be applied equally to the wine and the staff. I was unaware of it when I embarked upon my first tour of the Western Cape wine farms, but it is not acceptable to continue sampling the most expensive wines without showing some sort of indication that you are prepared to actually buy a bottle. Staff are trained to compile psychological profiles of everyone who walks in. But they can't watch us all. Make sure that you follow a tour group inside. While the French are hawking and spitting and generally behaving badly, you can get down twelve, maybe fifteen, glasses of the cheap stuff. Since the tots are a little on the teeny side, I have found that pouring five or six different wines into one glass often works best. Then you can sip at your leisure while the attendant refills the glasses that she thinks the greedy French have finished. Repeat until you are led out staggering and shouting about the time you were caught deep in Shiraz country with your trousers around your ankles and a donkey on your tail.

How to respond if a person of colour hits on you

Rule number one: Don't panic. First, ascertain the colour. With skin lighteners and tanning beds, it is becoming increasingly difficult to tell a person's race with any degree of certainty. The waters have been muddied and the lines blurred. You do not want to come across as politically incorrect, so do not, under any circumstances, refuse to go to bed with them, should they ask. However, if it turns out that they only want a few bob to buy a loaf of bread and a small house in Llandudno, then it is important to know which tribe they belong to. Should you fail to do so, you run the risk of responding in a fashion that will brand you a cultural anachronism, and even though you don't know what that means, you know it can't be good.

Remember that white is also a colour. Not a very impressive one, admittedly, but it is most definitely a colour, and should be treated as such. However, if you are black and a white person hits on you, this does not mean you should stab them in the eye with your swizzle stick and run like hell. They probably mean you no harm. You may, however, find that they are German or Swedish, but this shouldn't be a problem because black and white South Africans are still struggling to speak the same language. So you should feel quite at home.

How to avoid getting old

- Autoerotic asphyxiation.
- Swim naked at Gansbaai while a friend on a boat pours fish guts into the water around you.
- Cut a broomstick into six or seven equal lengths and

run towards an Israeli military checkpoint shouting in Arabic.
- Use embalming fluid instead of milk with your morning cereal.

How to drink and dive with panache

Drinking and diving is the new paralympic sport for athletes disabled in drink-driving accidents. They still get to drink, but all they need is a Speedo and a towel instead of a high-powered car. The water is softer than the concrete underpass that they rammed, and they still get to do somersaults, except this time off a diving board and not through the windscreen.

Pissoir etiquette

If you are alone and a man walks up and takes the urinal next to you, it is important to make a point of looking at his willy. This shows that you were there first and are in charge of the pissoir. He will get stage fright and will have to stand there pointlessly holding his willy in his hand until you zip up and leave. Again, it is important for you to hold your ground. Do not leave until he does. Even if you have finished your business, put your willy back in its pouch and stand there. The intruder knows that he cannot leave because that would mean never being able to show his face in those parts again. He also knows that he badly needs to go, but cannot because you are now standing there with your hands in your pockets making popping noises with your mouth and staring at the ice in the urinal.

Why all the pretty girls shop at Woolworths

This is true. In fact, I don't think ugs are even allowed in. If you are into ugs, try Shoprite. The place is full of them. Lovely warm women with great characters and faces like dogs' bums. They are often very friendly and smile at me in a non-threatening manner because they are accustomed to men not wanting to have sex with them. But go to Woolworths and you will see the difference. There, the nip 'n tuck brigade stalk the aisles with intent. When a woman makes lingering eye contact with you in Shoprite, you can be sure that she is in one of those thousand-yard stares that women get when they are wondering if the tuna is on special. But a woman who does this in Woolworths is asking to be roundly rogered in the fruit and veg section as soon as the manager turns his back. This doesn't happen to everyone, of course. Don't think you can buy your groceries at Shoprite and then stop off at Woolworths for a meat pie and a quick shag behind the kosher section. It doesn't work that way. You have to *belong*. And, believe me, these women know at a glance whether you belong. The simple act of picking up a basket marks you as an outsider. This tells the regular either that you don't have enough money for a full trolley of luxuries or, even worse, you live alone. And, while the married Woolworths woman is not morally opposed to the idea of a torrid affair, she would far rather have one with a man who is living with somebody. These women have based their entire lives on the principle of quid pro quo, or, in layman's terms, the goose and gander principle. Woolworths women also prefer to have their food neatly packaged and compartmentalised, just like their men. This is why when the aisles are suddenly invaded by an unruly brute with unshaven face and shirt hanging out, they become momentarily disoriented. Take advantage of their confusion. Wear reflective sunglasses and follow them about. This won't do much for you, but it gives them a thrill.

How to appear smarter than you really are

The main thing here is not to talk. Unless you are cross-eyed and dribbling with a traffic cone on your head, it is very difficult for anyone to gauge how intelligent you are merely by looking at you. Women have the edge, here. Nobody likes a woman who talks too much. Not even other women, but only because it cuts into their voice time. To get a man's attention, all a woman has to do is smile and drop her eyes. Not physically, of course. No man with the exception of the occasional German would be aroused by the sight of a woman's eyeballs rolling about the floor.

Sooner or later, men have to talk. They can carry the

strong, silent type thing for only so long. And, unlike women, they can't get away with flashing a bit of cleavage in lieu of an entire evening's conversation. So, if you are a man and you are particularly stupid, make sure that you have a few prepared quotes. If you are unable to memorise them, enter them into your cellphone and then, while pretending to check your messages, recite them. Here are a few you may wish to use:

- Did you know that mental illness is the second leading cause of disability and early death in the US and other developed countries?
- You have the most beautiful [insert feature] I have ever seen.
- What do you think Descartes really meant when he said: "*Cogito, ergo sum*"?
- Fancy a quick shag?

How to deal with road rage

First, you have to choose a weapon. It's no good snorting and saying, "Well, obviously," under your breath. Many, many drivers assume that they are prepared simply because they have grabbed whatever comes to hand and tossed it into the back of the car with absolutely no thought to the matter.

I know someone who keeps a pool noodle under his seat. When I asked him the reason, he said it was the first thing he saw in the garage. He claimed that he could disable me within thirty seconds using his noodle. When I laughed he became very defensive, and asked if he should go and fetch his noodle. I said that wouldn't be necessary. I wasn't about to take any chances. Perhaps he really has mastered a new art of Chinese noodle fighting.

Most people prefer the more conventional tools of the trade. Baseball bats, hockey sticks and pick handles are all popular among the Jetta and Polo set. BMW drivers tend to opt for more exotic implements, such as the short-handled Owambo war club, while Mercedes owners go for the more technologically advanced but less sporting snub-nosed Beretta.

I know this will offend a lot of people, but I find the baseball bat to be very clichéd. Every moron with a licence seems to think he is the first to come up with the idea. Personally, I wouldn't be caught dead assaulting anyone with a baseball bat, even if it is one of those fancy Tungsten ones. Now if you want to talk about a hand-carved *kliphout* knobkierie from the Lusikisiki area, that's another matter.

Knowing how to use your tool is almost as important as knowing which one to choose. Even young children think they know how to disable a careless driver with something as crude as a baseball bat. Pick it up and swing, right? Wrong! Like throwing a boomerang, it is all in the wrist action.

You also need to know what kind of injury you are going to inflict. Bludgeoning is passé. It not only leaves a terrible mess behind, but you also run the risk of pulling a muscle. The modern road-rager prefers to go for something a little tidier, such as a snapped tibia. There is also something very Zen about leaving behind nothing more than a pair of crushed metacarpals.

How to deal with rogue cops

First, it is important to remember that all cops are rogue cops. The only difference is that some are able to repress their dark side better than others. The urge to carry guns and handcuffs and interfere in everyone's lives is not a natural one. This is why it is always a good idea to treat the police with a great deal of circumspection. The hard-wiring in their brains is already out of whack, and it does not take a great deal of provocation to get them frothing at the mouth and scrabbling for weapons. In other words, talk to them as you would any other decent human being. The only difference is, do it as if you have a speech impediment. A great deal of fun can be had by talking to a policeman as if you were born with a harelip. Or you may wish to try a falsetto lisp. I have a friend who prefers to reverse his l's and r's. Police are not trained to deal with people who are clearly afflicted with some kind of terrible disorder that makes them sound like a cross between a steam train and a Chinese transvestite. If you have a car full of people, it is important that they do not burst out laughing as you spew your mangled words in the officer's general direction. It is best not to play this game if anybody in the car is stoned. I have found that people high on drugs are rarely able to contain their emotions in such situations. And there are few things more dangerous that a constable who realises that he is being mocked. So, rule number one is: Keep a straight face at all times.

Rogue cops can be dangerously unpredictable. That is why they are called rogue cops. One of the first things you may want to do on being confronted by a rogue cop is disarm him. This sounds harder than it actually is. The trick to getting his gun away from him is to get him to swallow six or seven Rohypnols. If you don't have any Rohypnols on you, I suppose you could use any other industrial-strength muscle relaxant. Nine times out of ten, the officer will immediately return to his car and take a long nap. Sometimes he will take a nap right next to your car in the middle of the street. The right thing to do is to drag him out of the road and make him comfortable on the pavement, or preferably down an embankment where nobody can see him. When he wakes he will feel refreshed and in a better mood, and you will be at home drinking cold beer and watching television. Everyone wins. Unfortunately, the lawyers have informed me that I am unable to give precise instructions on how to get the Rohypnol into the officer.

How to deal with New Age faith healers in public conveniences

New Age faith healers go around telling people stories like this: "Nicanor, a lame man, was sitting by the temple when a young boy ran up to him and snatched away his crutches.

Nicanor chased after the boy in hot pursuit and was cured." Then they stand back and look at you with a triumphant smile as if to say: "What more proof could you possibly want?"

Many people have had this kind of encounter. Bodger was one of them. Bodger was married to his stepsister's friend's cousin and spent some time in London, but then came back to South Africa. Bodger said he was standing at the trough in a public urinal in Margate when a man came up next to him and started telling him about the time when the infertile Agameda of Ceoa went to sleep in the temple, whereupon she dreamt of a serpent lying on her belly and five children were later born to her. Bodger is one of those men who find it impossible to go with another man standing right there, even if he is not saying anything. He said he ignored the man and tried to pretend that he was an engineer at a hydroelectric power station opening up a jammed valve, and was almost there when this stranger started recounting the story of a patient at the ancient Greek health spa, Epidaurus. He turned to Bodger and said: "When perchance my penis was hurt, I feared the surgeon's hands. I was reluctant to entrust my membrum virile to the care and the very great gods such as Phoebus and the son of Phoebus." Bodger says he has never been back to a public urinal. He says he goes in the bushes, or if there are no bushes around, he might go between two parked cars. Unless, of course, there is a street light right above him, in which case he says he tries to hold it until he gets home.

The point of the story is that New Age healers can be

found anywhere. And they do not take kindly to arguments. If, for instance, Bodger had said to this man that Agameda had no business being in a temple alone at night and that it's not surprising she encountered a lonely "serpent", it is very likely that the man would have sprayed Bodger's leg with urine and run off down the street.

Ignoring them rarely works because in their fevered minds, silence is a sign of kinship, and it only encourages them to try to reach you on a deeper level. If you are stuck next to someone who suddenly begins explaining the Tridosha theory to you, it is best that you interrupt and point out that Grigori Rasputin is your spiritual leader and that you are a high-ranking member of the Khlyst sect. Tell him you are a practised flagellant, and invite him back to your place for a good, healthy whipping. That should distract him long enough for you to reach the safety of a crowd.

How to cure your partner of jealousy

Jealousy is the strangest of all the crippling neuroses we have at our disposal. It is a destructive emotion that rears its viperous head in many different forms. Take penis envy, for instance. For a lot of men, this form of jealousy manifests itself when they find themselves standing at the pissoir alongside a man who is hung like a wildebeest. Even though it is considered very poor etiquette to steal a glance, there is very little else to look at in this situation. What these men don't realise, however, is that when Sigmund Freud spoke of penis envy, he had something altogether different in mind. Freud had a theory that the anatomical differences between the sexes lead every girl to envy every boy his possession of the penis. And, as she grows up, her wish to possess a penis turns into a wish to possess a man as the carrier of a penis. This, in turn, transforms itself into something even more complex, involving the holding of grudges against other women for their possession of men (and their penises, I presume). Freud was clearly out of his mind.

Modern psychology proposes a number of different ways of curing your partner of jealousy, but I have always found the most effective method to be the .357 Magnum, although these days most women prefer the less cumbersome but equally effective 9-mm Glock. It looks like a toy, but the women I have spoken to swear it works like a charm. One well-placed shot and, voila, no more jealousy.

How to get the best out of your drugs

It is important to remember that drugs are like electrical appliances. A grey product, whether it be heroin or a waffle iron, can kill you.

A popular misconception is that all drugs make you high. They do not. Some make you so low that you cannot even look your dog in the eye. This is why so many teenagers become disillusioned and cynical. The dealer on the corner says, "Hey, pssst, wanna get high?' and then sells them something that dumps them on level four of Dante's Inferno.

Lysergic acid diethylamide is a bit like a child with Down's syndrome in that it is difficult to look after and can go off quite quickly. It is important to remember that not all types of LSD react the same way. Superman, for example, becomes more powerful if left in direct sunlight for eight hours, while Goofy is at its best after two days in the fridge. It all comes down to acid management, really.

Cocaine, sprinkled lightly on well-browned lasagne, is absolutely divine. But remember to use imported Italian pasta and not that dreadful fake stuff churned out in the southern industrial area.

Marijuana, South Africa's primary export crop, is one of the most versatile ingredients that you could hope to find at the back of your underwear drawer. It can be snorted like snuff, used to garnish a roast chicken or even as a substitute for catnip to keep your new kittens amused for hours on end.

Ketamine is much like truffles in that it is very hard to find out of season. You may want to try your local vet, or even the stables if you have some nearby. Horse tranquillisers are among the most effective in their group, and have been known to quieten down even the most neurotic of Johannesburg kugels. Racehorses rarely misbehave, and there is no reason why you should, either.

Psilocybin is absolutely delicious when fried up with a few rashers of back bacon, a handful of wild tomatoes, and three or four free-range eggs. Wake up early on a Sunday morning and surprise your loved one with a tray of these earthy delights. He or she will thank you in many new and interesting ways. Go on, put the fun back in fungus!

Heroin should be avoided because it is just plain immoral to buy anything from Afghanistan now that America has taken over the drug trade.

Methylenedioxymethamphetamine, street slang for Ecstasy, is hard to beat when it comes to chasing away those Monday morning blues. Washed down with a glass of fresh orange juice, you'll find the day simply flying by in a warm, fuzzy blur of contentment.

Beer, like a dead body, should be kept on ice at all times. At breakfast time, it makes a refreshing change from mango juice and always goes well with a fish lunch. Some say that beer itself makes the ideal lunch, but I believe that you should always snack on something while drinking beer. That way, when you develop an enormous gut, you can always blame the peanuts.

What to do if your girlfriend is a barmaid

Unless you are a rabid teetotaller with right-wing fundamentalist tendencies, the chances are that you have fantasised about having a relationship with the woman who works behind the bar in your local pub. Or any pub, for that matter. This is quite normal and you have nothing to worry about. Unless, of course, she is one of those chain-smoking bartenders with stringy hair, elephantine thighs and a furtive addiction to cheap brandy. Then you should be worried.

The advantages of having a bartender girlfriend far outweigh the disadvantages. To make full use of this rare opportunity, it is strongly advisable that you spend as much time in the bar as possible. You will never again have such a watertight case for going to the bar night after night.

Order as many drinks from her as possible. It is her job to bring them to you and, unlike when she is at home with you, she is not allowed to refuse. Stockpile if you have to, but whenever she gets a breather between serving other people, shout at the top of your voice: "Bartender! Another pint of your finest!" Then, when she brings it to you, lean quickly over the bar counter and kiss her full on the lips. This will drive the other patrons into a frenzy of envy. The danger, here, is that they will all start trying it, and the next thing you know you are up on the bar with your stool in one hand and a broken bottle in the other, threatening to disembowel the next man who touches your girl. It might be wiser not to kiss her at all. Anyway, there is a very good chance that kissing her will affect her tips in a big way.

If a customer catches you with your tongue in the bartender's mouth, he is going to correctly assume that something is not quite kosher. And, if he suspects that he has a less than zero chance of getting jiggy with her, he will see little point in tipping her after every drink. She needs her tips. So do you. In fact, you may want to set a precedent by giving her ridiculously large tips after every drink in the hope that everyone else will feel guilty enough to do the same. You can always get your money back later when she is asleep. Something happens to men's brains when they walk into a bar. I have seen it happen countless times. Their tips grow progressively larger as the evening wears on, as if somehow a magical number will be reached whereby the bartender will drop her tray and say: "Oh, baby, you're such a great tipper. Please come home with me!" I have only seen this happen once in my life, and I can tell you that the circumstances on that occasion were far from normal.

When she is off duty but you find yourself in the bar, anyway, it is important to avoid flirting with any of the girls there. The law of averages states that you, your bartender girlfriend and the flirtee will, on any given evening, all appear in the bar at the same time. You girlfriend will be baffled by your sudden inclination not to talk, move or look anywhere else but at the bottle of imported rum on the bottom shelf. The flirtee will be baffled that you are ignoring her after having spent so much time buying her drinks and feigning interest in her life story just a week ago. And you, you will just be plain baffled. It is a terrible situation to be in, and short of a fire breaking out in the kitchen, there is no escape. Leaving suddenly is certain to arouse the suspicions of the barmaid. Besides, you do not want to run the risk of leaving the flirtee and your girlfriend alone in the same room. What can happen if you quietly slip out the back is that the flirtee, having seen that you are on friendly terms with the girl behind the bar, will approach her and say: "Hi. That cute guy who just walked out. He came on to me the other night and I never got his name. Do you know what it is?" By the time she gets home you are in bed pretending to be asleep. Do not be surprised to find that your name is now "Bastard".

How to win the Argus/ Pick 'n Pay Cycle Tour

The first thing you should know about this race is that the route is a very difficult one. However, there are certain parts that will make it a lot easier for you to finish, and even win, this race. My favourite is a cul-de-sac at the bottom of Queens Road in Sea Point. From here to the finish line is a mere 3.5 kilometres. There is a large bush growing on a traffic island at the entrance to the cul-de-sac. If you are careful and get there early enough, none of the race organisers will spot you. Then it's just a matter of waiting for the race leaders to swing out of Victoria Road into Queens, and then it's a sharp right at the traffic circle and into Beach Road, the home stretch. Because of the hairpin bend, riders are preoccupied with making the turn and spectators are busy silently willing someone to crash. Nobody will notice as you slip out from behind the bush and join the frontrunners. A word of advice: Come in at the back. This is very important. If you suddenly appear in front of someone who has risked his heart and genitals to keep the lead for the last 100 kilometres, he will not be as accommodating as you might think.

It is just as important to decide well beforehand what drugs you are going to take. Narco-loading is vital for racers such as us. Essentially, we are sprinters. And jumping into the race two hours after the official start is not as easy as it sounds. For a start, the drugs will make you thirsty. I have always found that two plastic bottles, one holding white wine and the other red, can clip neatly onto the frame of any of the more expensive models. If wine is too pretentious for you, I suggest you make use of one of those cunning backpacks that are designed to hold a litre bottle of pre-mixed Jose Cuervo and orange juice. It is easy enough to run a plastic tube from the bottle to the mouth.

Ideal race drugs include Dexedrine (to get the heart rate up), ketamine (to verbally abuse your fellow competitors) and LSD (to brighten up the colours). Just remember that while narco-loading is great for short sprints, one of the side effects is that you see and hear things that might not altogether exist. If you finish the race and claim victory, there may be a lot of angry people in yellow vests who will try to convince you otherwise. Whether or not you listen to them is up to you.

If you are a man, you might also want to think about rolling up a pair of socks and putting them down your lycra shorts. Sportsmen are always held in higher esteem when people see that they are hauling serious freight. If you are arrested at any time during or after the race, be sure to remove the socks before entering the police cell.

How to behave when impersonating a doctor

I am not sure why, but it is apparently illegal to masquerade as a doctor. On the other hand, it is quite legal to impersonate a journalist. It makes no sense to me. If you visit a doctor or speak to a journalist, you are quite literally putting your life in their hands. But while a journalist might destroy your reputation, a doctor can do little more than cause you physical harm.

Besides, untrained and unqualified doctors would be a whole lot cheaper than some of those heartless greedheads out there who think the world owes them a living just because they are legally entitled to render you unconscious and then slice you up like you were some kind of prime beef.

Bastards.

When deciding to impersonate someone in the medical profession, it will be quite tempting to pretend to be a surgeon. There is something about all that scrubbing up and snapping on of rubber gloves that appeals to a suprising number of men (17.2%) and women (0.1%). However, I strongly suggest that you choose to impersonate someone else. Surgeons are regularly called upon to perform surgery. This is why they are called surgeons. And, unless you know your spleen from your pancreas, it is best to stay away from the operating theatre. Besides, most men (87.5%) know so little about the workings of the female body that they could not be trusted with a naked, drugged woman lying on a table in front of them. Especially not with a razor-sharp scalpel in their hands. Women impersonators, too, should avoid a similar situation involving male patients, especially if they suffer from penis envy.

It is, however, easy enough to impersonate a general practitioner and move through the wards in a white coat and stethoscope feeling patients' foreheads and making them laugh with your comically exaggerated invoices. But keep it professional. You do not want to be mistaken for Patch Adams.

If you are a man, you might want to be among the 0.3% of men who impersonate gynaecologists. This is the dream job of most adolescent boys. It is only when they grow up that they realise this is not at all what they want from life. There is no rational explanation for this, particularly when you consider that a mechanic will work on a Porsche Carrera all day long and when it comes time to knock off he will get into his Nissan Sentra and drive home without complaining once. Perhaps there are fundamental differences between cars and women that should be taken into account here.

Research undertaken by nobody who wants to come forward and take credit for it has shown that it is far more fulfilling to impersonate a doctor of the mind. The good thing about pretending to be a head doctor is that you can operate from your home and you do not need much in the way of specialised equipment. A couch, a box of tissues and a notebook and pen should cover it. If you have one, a video camera can liven things up a bit. If you do this properly, it won't be long before you develop a healthy list of unhealthy patients. There is really only one thing to remember when treating mentally ill people: do not laugh at them. Ever. Do not even try to laugh with them. If they start laughing, excuse yourself and leave the room until they have stopped. The sounds you are looking for are mewling and sobbing. Only then can you do your job properly.

Diagnosing people with psychiatric problems is a lot easier than you think. For a start, they hardly ever argue with you because they genuinely believe that they are sick and you aren't. This gives you an edge right from the start. If you are ever at a loss for words, all you have to do is rub your chin, look out the window, nod slowly and mumble. It doesn't really matter what you mumble because most of the time the patient will be too afraid to ask you to repeat it. If they do ask, however, you could say something like: "It's the Aubert-Fleischl paradox. Hmm. Very interesting. Very interesting indeed…" The patient will not press you for details because they already fear for their sanity and would far rather not know about the Aubert-Fleischl paradox.

Developing your own Rorschach test can also be a lot of fun. In fact, if you have young children, you might get them to play around with a bottle of ink and a few pages of blotting paper. See what they come up with, then pass them on to your patients for their interpretation. At the very least the family will have a good laugh around the dinner table. If you are trying to get rid of a problem patient (i.e. one who never pays on time), you might suggest that at your next session you will explain the Whorfian hypothesis as it relates to his condition. He won't be back.

If a patient's symptoms make no sense whatsoever (e.g. biting the edge of your desk, urinating in your wastepaper bin), do not be alarmed. Have a little sport. The best way of passing the time in extreme situations is to tell the patient that he is suffering from a range of phobias. Ask him to subtract 1 from 14. If he runs into the wall screaming, tell him he has triskaidekaphobia. When he has calmed down, tell him you have detected signs of dysmorphophobia. Don't tell him what it means. He will find out on his own and will never again be able to look into a mirror. There are many more. Keep going until he signs up for another twenty sessions. If you have done your job properly, he will have developed phobophobia, the fear of acquiring a phobia, by the time he leaves.

If a patient confronts you with suspicions that you are an impersonator, laugh easily and tell him that this is understandable because you subscribe to the Gestalt psychology movement, and people often make the same mistake. Once he discovers that there is no English equivalent for the word "gestalt", he will have no option but to give you the benefit of the doubt. He already suspects he is going mad, and will not want to appear stupid on top of it.

How to be a sex tourist while training for the Kololi Pool Challenge in the Gambia

Some people think that sex tourism is all there is to the Gambia. This is not true. There is also the Kololi Pool Challenge that takes place once a year. Or once a week, depending on the number of entries. And the rainy season. And the groundnut harvest.

The best way to prepare for the tournament is to become a sex tourist. I have always found that if you choose a short, heavy cue and a tall, light-skinned woman, you stand a damn good chance of winning. Most of your opponents will be Rastafarians. They play with heads full of powerful Gambian weed, but do not be lulled into a false sense of security just because they have to be reminded whether they are stripes or solids after each shot. Your opponents will also be attached to some of the biggest, scariest women you will ever come across in your life. Try not to be intimidated. They are sex tourists just like you, except they are from Dusseldorf and Wapping.

It is important that you learn some basic Wolof so that you can order beers and women throughout the challenge. You do not want to run dry of either. This will give your opponents the edge. Here is a helpful phrase I picked up while defending my title a few years ago: "Danka danka mojapa golo sinjai." It means "slowly, slowly catchee monkey". Or, "slowly, slowly catchee syphilis". One of the two.

How to deal with a woman who wears fur coats

Try to get her into bed as quickly as possible. Women who wear fur are animalistic and violent, but even better than that, they are frequently very rich.

However, if she refuses to sleep with you, there are several ways in which to respond. You may want to buy a gram or so of PCP (angel dust) and follow her home. Sneak into the garden when she is in her bedroom biting the legs off baby mice or whatever it is that women who wear fur and won't sleep with us do when they are alone. Wrap the PCP in a pork sausage and feed it to her dog when it comes out to bark at you. Two hours later, when she bends down to kiss her beloved pooch goodnight, its little brain will be about ready to snap its moorings. Try not to laugh as she runs from the house with a Maltese poodle latched to her throat like some kind of avante-garde accessory from the House of Pain.

What to do if your partner has an aversion to bathing

This is essentially a male trait, but I have encountered women who suffer from what I regard as a deviant version of hydrophobia.

There was one woman in particular who resolutely refused to shower or bath, regardless of how much money I offered her. I tried to find out the reason once or twice, but

I never really made an issue out of it because some women are sensitive to interrogation. In the end, I gave up trying to convince her that soap and water are not the twin pillars of evil, and instead began licking her clean. It was fun while it lasted, but it is not something I would recommend on any long-term basis.

However, should you find yourself married to such a person, there are a number of tongue exercises that you can do. Tie a piece of string to the top of a full beer bottle and wrap the other end tightly around the base of your tongue. Now hang your head down as if you are about to throw up. Retract your tongue slowly and then let it out again. Do this fifty times while taking short, shallow breaths, like a dog panting on a hot day. This will develop your diaphragm and give you the necessary stamina to lick your woman from head to toe at least three times a week.

Look. I could keep going for another five years. But, like I said, these mercenary swine are on my tail and they will not hesitate to send me to jail if I do not hand over a stiffy disk to them by midday tomorrow.

If your life has taken a turn for the worse since reading this book, please do not hesitate to let my publishers know.

Bastards.